5-05

W9-CFB-971

BRITAIN

Barbara Fuller

BENCHMARK BOOKS

MARSHALL CAVENDISH
NEW YORK

PICTURE CREDITS
Cover photo: © Alamy Images: Medioimages
Bridgeman Art Library: 92 • Derek Cattani/Eye Ubiquitous: 52 • Corel Stock Photo Library: 53, 57 • Bennett
Dean/Eye Ubiquitous: 42 • Food Features: 130, 131 • Hulton-Deutsch Collection: 22, 23, 24, 26, 31, 32, 79,
95, 97, 101 • Hutchison Library: 33, 35, 43, 45, 67, 70, 96, 112 • Image Bank: 7, 14, 16, 40, 44, 48, 98, 103,
108 • International Photobank: 6, 9, 54, 116 • Sakina Kadga: 89 • Life File Photo Library: 8, 10, 11, 12, 13,
25, 27, 36, 46, 49, 64, 65, 68, 69, 71, 72, 74, 75, 77, 80, 99, 102, 107, 109, 110, 111, 114, 117, 121, 123, 125,
128 • Lonely Planet Images: 15 • Paul Massey/Hutchison Library: 5 • Photo Disc: 51, 55 • David Simson: 18,
59, 63, 90, 93, 122 • Michael Spilling: 21 • Sylvia Cordaiy Photo Library: 1, 50, 124 • Liba Taylor: 3, 4, 61, 73,
82, 83, 85, 113, 119 • Liba Taylor/Hutchison Library: 76 • Travel Ink Ltd: 34 • Nik Wheeler: 20, 58, 66, 84,
104 • John Wright: 17, 38, 41, 47, 60, 81, 88, 94, 106, 115, 118, 129 • Peter Wright: 19, 105

ACKNOWLEDGMENTS
Thanks to Ruth Mitchell-Pitts PhD, Associate Director, Center for European Studies, University of North
Carolina at Chapel Hill for her expert reading of this manuscript.

PRECEDING PAGE
A British family on a picnic in a park.

Marshall Cavendish Benchmark
99 White Plains Road
Tarrytown, NY 10591
Website: www.marshallcavendish.us

© Times Media Private Limited 1996, 1994
© Marshall Cavendish International (Asia) Private Limited 2005
All rights reserved. First edition 1994. Second edition 2005.

® "Cultures of the World" is a registered trademark of Marshall Cavendish Corporation.

Originated and designed by Times Editions
An imprint of Marshall Cavendish International (Asia) Private Limited
A member of Times Publishing Limited

Library of Congress Cataloging-in-Publication Data
Fuller, Barbara, 1961-
    Britain / by Barbara Fuller.— 2nd ed.
        p. cm. — (Cultures of the world)
    Summary: "Explores the geography, history, government, people, and culture of
        Britain"—Provided by publisher.
    Includes bibliographical references and index.
    ISBN 0-7614-1845-8
    1. Great Britain—Juvenile literature. I. Title. II. Series: Cultures of the world (2nd ed.)
    DA27.5.F85 2005
    941—dc22   2004027498

Printed in China

7 6 5 4 3 2 1

CONTENTS

The handsome uniform of
the Queen's personal
guards.

3

Costumes worn at the annual Lord Mayor's Show.

INTRODUCTION

The British Isles, of which Britain is the largest island, were part of the continent of Europe until about 80 million years ago. The geology clearly links the eastern coast with neighboring Scandinavia. Since 1994 Britain has been linked to Europe once more, this time by the 31-mile (50-km) Channel Tunnel rail link.

Britain consists of the three countries of England, Scotland, and Wales, all of which are under the same political system. Together with Northern Ireland, it is part of the United Kingdom that belongs to the European Union of 25 countries. Britain still retains its own currency (pounds and pence), rather than adopting the European Union's currency, the euro, which came into force in 2002.

Historically and politically, Britain has strong ties with the United States. After the terrorist attacks of September 11, 2001, British prime minister Tony Blair was quick to show support for U.S. president George Bush.

GEOGRAPHY

BRITAIN IS LOCATED between 50° and 60° north latitude, and at 0° longitude. It is 600 miles (967 km) at its longest point from the north of Scotland to the southern coast of England, and 300 miles (483 km) at its widest point from the west of Wales to the eastern coast. England is 50,350 square miles (130,410 square km) in area; Scotland is 30,420 square miles (78,790 square km); and Wales is 8,020 square miles (20,760 square km). Britain's total population is approximately 60.3 million, mostly concentrated in the southeast, particularly in the Greater London area.

Above: **The white cliffs of Dover in the county of Kent on the southeastern coast.**

Opposite: **A village in Somerset, England.**

The British Isles were separated from the continent of Europe at the end of the last Ice Age, when temperatures rose and the ice cap melted, flooding the shallow shelf of what is now the North Sea and the English Channel.

PHYSICAL GEOGRAPHY

The main geological structures of Europe continue westward to Britain: the great plain of northern Europe reappears as the windswept lowlands of eastern England, and north of these lowlands are remnants of Scandinavian mountains split by rift valleys. The fjords of Norway are repeated in the indented western Scottish coasts; *ria* (ree-ah) coasts (coastal inlets) like those of Spain and Brittany are found in South Wales; the German and Dutch estuaries and shores are echoed in eastern England, with submerged river mouths and wide shallow bays; and the white cliffs of Dover in Kent mirror those of Picardy in France, only 20 miles (32 km) away across the English Channel. Britain's highlands lie in the north and west, with a central belt of lowlands farther east.

EAST ANGLIA Norfolk, Suffolk, Cambridgeshire, and Essex make up Britain's eastern bulge, known as East Anglia. Rarely rising above 300 feet (91 m), the drained fens and broken-down glacial deposits make fertile arable land. This region has the lowest annual rainfall in the country. Norwich and Cambridge are historic cities in the region.

THE SOUTH COAST The chalk ridges of Kent's North Downs and Sussex's South Downs run parallel in an east-west direction and are broken by north- or south-flowing streams. They face inward over the Weald, a concentric series of clay valleys and sandstone ridges. The Hampshire Basin is ringed by chalk hills. Coastal resort towns include Bognor Regis and Brighton. Canterbury in Kent has England's main Anglican cathedral.

THE HOME COUNTIES London's suburban sprawl stretches out toward more picturesque villages in the surrounding counties. The Chiltern Hills rise to over 800 feet (244 m) and have colorful beech woods. The valley of the Thames river extends from the river's source in Gloucestershire through Henley-on-Thames to the royal castle at Windsor and beyond to London.

THE WEST COUNTRY The monoliths of Stonehenge are a popular tourist attraction on the chalk downs of Salisbury Plain. Dorset's moody countryside of pastures and barren heaths is described in the novels of Thomas Hardy, while the limestone and fossils of Lulworth Cove on the coast are a geologist's dream. Devon's pretty coastal towns contrast with the classic

The Norfolk Broads are the result of 12th-century peat cutting. People used this decayed marsh vegetation for fuel when other resources were scarce. Over 2,500 acres (1,012 hectares) were dug up during this period. Today it is a popular holiday center for boating enthusiasts from all over Britain.

granite moorlands of Exmoor and Dartmoor, which have rocky tors (pinnacles) and upland plateaus. The Cornish coast is more rugged than Devon's and is a popular tourist area. The Eden Project in Bodelva, which is a chain of interconnecting greenhouses containing plants from around the world, opened in 2001. It is a major tourist attraction in Cornwall.

On the northern edge of the Somerset Plain are the Mendip Hills where Cheddar Gorge—famous for caving, rock climbing, and cheese production—is located.

Golden-colored oolite stone makes for picturesque towns and villages in the Cotswolds, such as Burford and Oxford. Bath is an 18th-century spa town; its thermal baths date from Roman times.

England's largest natural lake, Lake Windermere, is in the popular Lake District.

WALES The principality of Wales is 135 miles (217 km) long and 35 miles (56 km) wide. The Black Mountains and the Brecon Beacons are rugged mountainous regions of South Wales, the latter rising to about 2,660 feet (811 m). The coast of Pembrokeshire is a national park, home to numerous seabirds. Cardiff and Swansea are major cities of South Wales.

Most of the uplands of Central Wales are drained by the Wye river. To the east, the Welsh plateau breaks up into the Welsh border hills, cut through by the Severn Valley.

North Wales is more agricultural than the south. Sheep farming is the most effective use of this area characterized by high and glaciated uplands. Mount Snowdon is 3,560 feet (1,085 m) high, accessible by mountain railway as well as by walking trails. Welsh knitwear and woven fabrics from the upland regions are renowned for their quality.

THE MIDLANDS Much of Britain's industrial development took place in the low plateaus of the Midlands, particularly in the areas near the Nottingham and Leicester coalfields known as the Black Country. The

industrial heritage of the area has become an important tourist and educational attraction. Coventry was a center of the automobile industry. Near Telford, the Ironbridge Gorge Museums have an interesting collection of industrial inventions. Warwick Castle, dating from the 14th century, is one of England's most important medieval castles. Stratford-upon-Avon, Shakespeare's birthplace, boasts Tudor-style black-and-white buildings, as well as the renowned Royal Shakespeare Company's Swan Theatre.

THE PEAK DISTRICT Britain's first national park, a horseshoe ring of sandstone ridge surrounding a limestone plateau with rivers flowing southeast, is bordered by Nottingham, Stoke-on-Trent, Greater Manchester, and Sheffield. Its wild moorlands and craggy rocks are popular with climbers and walkers. The 268-mile-(431-km-) long Pennine Way footpath starts here.

Northwest of the Peak District lies Lancashire; to its east over the Pennine Hills is Yorkshire. An age-old rivalry between the counties, based on two families' claims to the English throne, dates from the 15th century.

Warwick Castle in Warwickshire, near Coventry. Most of the present building dates back to the 14th and 15th centuries. Owned by the Tussauds Group (who also run the nearby theme park Alton Towers), Warwick Castle frequently features jousting displays and characters dressed in medieval costume.

Loch Ness. The earliest known reference to the Loch Ness monster was in Saint Adamman's biography of Saint Columba in the seventh century. Interest revived in the 1930s, and sporadic attempts to photograph or find the monster continue.

THE NORTHEAST County Durham lies on a coalfield, with steel and other heavy industries in Consett. It is also traversed by the rugged moorlands of the Pennines. Durham is a medieval university town, centered around a cathedral on a steep hill encircled by a river. Newcastle-upon-Tyne, once an important shipbuilding port, is now a vibrant cultural city, epitomized by its Gateshead Millennium Bridge. To the north of Newcastle lies Northumbria, where Hadrian's Wall, completed in A.D. 128, stretches for 73 miles (117 km) across England from Wallsend, Tyne and Wear to Bowness-on-Solway. Sheep farming and forestry are the main forms of agriculture in the region.

SCOTLAND Scotland's Southern Uplands encompass the border area and the southern region with undulating pastoral farming land. Farther north, the large cities of Edinburgh on the Firth of Forth on the eastern coast and Glasgow on the west, are sited 45 miles (72 km) apart at Scotland's narrowest neck. These cities are in the Central Lowlands that reach up to the Sidlaw and Ochil hills of Strathmore.

THE LAKE DISTRICT

This area, a mountainous region of radial hills interspersed with glaciated lake-filled troughs north of Lancashire in north-western England, attracts tourists year-round. Lake Windermere is popular for pleasure cruises and boating activities. Climbers attempt the 3,210-foot (980-m) Scafell Pike, or the lesser peaks of Skiddaw or Helvellyn. Hikers abound in this picturesque region.

The Grampian mountains form the division between the Lowlands and the Highlands in Scotland. Aberdeen is an important oil-processing town for the North Sea oil and gas fields. The islands of Jura and Islay, to the north of the Firth of Clyde, are renowned whiskey-producing areas; thick woolen knitwear comes from the nearby Island of Arran. Cut into the highland plateau, large glens—bleak and almost barren valleys—often have cool lakes called *lochs* (locks). Loch Ness, stretching in a southwest direction through Glen More from near Inverness on the eastern coast toward Fort Augustus, is reputed to harbor a prehistoric monster. Britain's highest mountain, the 4,406-foot (1,343-m) Ben Nevis, is near the lake.

To the north of Glen More lie the North West Highlands, where the population density drops to 6 persons per square mile (2.5 per square km). In the uplands many people are tenant farmers. On small farms of 5 to 10 acres (2 to 4 hectares), they grow oats and potatoes and keep chickens. Besides farming, knitwear and tweed manufacture are the local industries, while salmon and trout fishing, grouse shooting, and deer hunting are lucrative tourist attractions as well as popular pastimes for residents.

Tower Bridge spans the Thames east of the City of London, near the Tower of London. The bridge was completed in 1894; the lower section opens to allow large ships to pass below.

CITIES

Britain's cities act as regional and cultural centers, important places for business and tourism.

LONDON Britain's capital city is a center of international trade and finance, tourism, retailing, media, and government services. The area known as the City of London is the financial center. Located within its square mile are the Bank of England, the Stock Exchange, Lloyd's of London (insurance underwriters), and the headquarters of major banks. To the east of this area lies the Tower of London; farther east is the East End, formerly a center of the textile industry. The financial area has now been expanded eastward into the Canary Wharf development in the Docklands, a highly sought-after office and residential location.

In contrast, the West End is the entertainment district. Many theaters are located near Piccadilly Circus and Shaftesbury Avenue; Leicester Square has numerous movie theaters; Oxford Street and nearby streets are shopping areas; and Covent Garden has a prestigious opera house and a flourishing handicrafts market.

The Houses of Parliament overlook the Thames in Westminster. A large clock tower commonly referred to as Big Ben (which is actually the name of the bell in the tower) rises on the north side of the building. Westminster Abbey, located across the street, was founded by King Edward the Confessor in 1065. Government offices and ministries are found in Whitehall, with the residences of the prime minister and the

chancellor of the exchequer on Downing Street. The Mall leads from Trafalgar Square to Buckingham Palace. The British Museum and University College London are in the Bloomsbury area between the West End and the City.

BIRMINGHAM Birmingham is a center of finance and professional services, home to one of Europe's largest conference centers and Europe's largest electronics organization, as well as other light and medium industries, such as metals and engineering, automobiles and bicycles, and machine tools. The city has three universities and its own symphony orchestra.

MANCHESTER Manchester has a population of about 400,000, but 2.5 million live in Greater Manchester. The city became wealthy in Victorian times, deriving its wealth from the cotton trade and its associated industries. Today it is a regional banking center and the home of the Northern Stock Exchange.

Crowds relaxing at the amphitheater outside the Great Northern cinema in Manchester.

After a severe economic decline during the 1970s when key manufacturing and shipbuilding industries were virtually destroyed, Glasgow has emerged to become a vibrant cultural and tourism center. In 1990 it was named a "City of Culture" by the European Union.

EDINBURGH Edinburgh Castle dominates the Scottish capital. It overlooks the Royal Mile, a street of beautiful 16th- and 17th-century townhouses that runs from the castle to the Palace of Holyroodhouse, the Queen's official Scottish residence. Edinburgh has three universities and a growing computer industry. Other industries include engineering, food processing, alcoholic beverages, tobacco, printing, and electrical goods. It is also a center for medicine, banking, insurance, tourism, and law, and acts as a marketplace for Scottish beef and salmon.

GLASGOW Scotland's largest city has a population of about 609,000. Its industries include textiles, food and beverages, engineering, and printing. The Glasgow School of Art, the 12th-century Glasgow Cathedral, and the renowned Burrell Collection of art are major tourist attractions.

CARDIFF The capital city of Wales, known as Caerdydd in Welsh, used to be a major port for exporting coal and steel. While these heavy industries have declined, Cardiff is now a service center for financial, insurance, and banking institutions, home to the Welsh Assembly, and a center for food processing and light engineering. The Millennium Stadium is a British national arena that seats 75,000 people for rugby and soccer competitions.

RIVERS

THE THAMES The Thames rises in the Cotswolds in Gloucestershire and flows to the North Sea at Tilbury 210 miles (338 km) to the east. It winds through picturesque scenery until it reaches London. The Thames is used for a variety of boating activities. Rowing competitions are regularly held on the river at Henley, Oxford, and Eton, while the annual Boat Race on the Thames in London between teams from Oxford and Cambridge universities is a major highlight.

London's position on the river makes it ideally suited as a port; the Thames below Tower Bridge is an extremely important waterway. Large container ships dock farther downriver at Tilbury since they cannot pass the Thames Flood Barrier (*below*), which was opened in 1984 to prevent the flooding of London by an unusually high tide. The Dartford Tunnel that runs beneath the Thames and the parallel overhead bridge complete London's orbital motorway called the M25.

THE SEVERN The Severn rises in North Wales and runs through the border country with Wales before reaching the Bristol Channel estuary. Its tidal range can be as much as 40 feet (12 m) during spring tides. The Severn Bridge over the river just north of Bristol is a major road link between England and Wales as well as an engineering triumph. Built in the 1960s, the bridge is 16,955 feet (5,168 m) long and spans 1,496 feet (456 m).

CLIMATE

Britain enjoys a cool to mild temperate climate with few extremes of temperature. The greatest variation in weather is in the southeast, but throughout Britain, temperatures rarely exceed 90°F (32°C) in summer or fall below 14°F (-10°C) in winter.

The Gulf Stream, a warm ocean current that crosses the Atlantic Ocean, produces warmer winters in the west of the country so that in January northwestern Scotland can be considerably warmer than southeastern England. Warm and wet westerly winds prevail, and since most upland areas are in the northern and western parts of the country, it is these regions that have the heaviest rainfall: over 60 inches (152 cm) annually, mainly in the fall and winter, compared with a national average of 40 inches (102 cm).

Mild winters and high rainfall in the west make the region well suited for livestock farming. By contrast, the sunny summers and flatter land in the east are more suited for arable farming. Throughout Britain the weather is always unpredictable, and therefore always a subject for conversation.

FLORA AND FAUNA

Britain has a diverse range of flora and fauna, despite increasing urbanization. Ten national parks in England and Wales conserve different types of rural environments. The uplands boast heather-strewn grouse moors, brackens, and a spiny evergreen shrub known as gorse. Wild roses and hawthorns flourish in southern England, wild daffodils herald spring in Yorkshire and the Lake District, and bluebell woods flourish in the Home Counties. There are 150 different types of grass in the British Isles. The English oak is abundant in forests such as Savernake Forest in Wiltshire and Sherwood Forest in Nottinghamshire, beechwoods are found in the Chilterns, and pine forests abound in Scotland.

Wild deer and ponies are found in Hampshire's New Forest (*below*); deer are found in some other woods, including areas of the West County and in the Scottish Highlands. Foxes, otters, bats, badgers, and field mice have adapted to the urban environment and are found throughout Britain. The red robin is a popular and territorial garden bird. Coastal areas and plowed arable land attract seagulls and hawks, while the larger birds of prey soar over highlands and even freeways in search of food. The peregrine falcon and the ptarmigan are found in the Scottish Highlands. Gray seals are common in underpopulated coastal areas. Brown trout and grayling are often found in rivers, while salmon and eel spend most of their lives at sea but return to spawn in rivers.

THE HISTORY OF PEOPLE in Britain stretches back for over 5,000 years. Barrows—communal burial grounds on the chalk uplands of southern England— are remnants of Britain's earliest Neolithic people, who arrived from the Iberian peninsula and parts of western Europe in about 3000 B.C. The Beaker people (so called because of their pottery skills) built hill forts, cultivated barley, and were buried in individual graves from around 2400 B.C.

From 700 B.C., different tribes of Celts arrived from Central Europe, bringing with them the knowledge of ironworking that revolutionized agriculture. They established hill forts and trade outlets on

the Thames and Firth of Forth. Their society was stratified and included a caste of Druid priests and a ruling warrior class.

The Romans invaded Britain in A.D. 43 and occupied the south of Britain from the Humber to the Severn rivers. They established garrison towns to watch over upland areas they did not control and brought Christianity to Britain. Boudicca, female leader of the Iceni (an ancient tribe that occupied present-day Norfolk), tried to drive the Romans out in A.D. 61 but was unsuccessful. The Romans failed to conquer Caledonia (now Scotland), so the Emperor Hadrian built a wall from coast to coast in the north of England to prevent incursions of Picts and Scots across the border. The last Roman troops left Britain around A.D. 410.

Above: **A statue of the legendary Boudicca in Colchester.**

Opposite: **The Stonehenge monument was first built around 3000 B.C. It is a World Heritage Site and is an extremely popular tourist destination.**

Vikings were sea rovers and pirates from present-day Scandinavia. They ravaged the coasts of Europe from the eighth to the 10th centuries.

THE ANGLO-SAXONS

Three Germanic tribes invaded soon after the Romans left. The Angles settled in the east, the Saxons farther west and in the northern Midlands, and the Jutes in Kent and the South Coast, driving the Celts farther north and west. The Anglo-Saxons founded the different kingdoms of Essex, Sussex, Wessex, Middlesex, East Anglia, Northumbria, and Mercia. Anglo-Saxon kings included King Offa of Mercia (reign 757 to 796), who built a long dike on the Welsh borders to keep the Celts at bay, and King Alfred of Wessex (Alfred the Great, 871–99), who used educated churchmen to draw up laws. It was also in Alfred's reign that the *Anglo Saxon Chronicle,* an extensive record of Britain's early history, was first written. Monks from the Scottish island Iona and the Northumbrian island Lindisfarne continued to spread the Christian religion. In the late sixth century, the monk Augustine became Britain's first Archbishop of Canterbury.

In 865 the Vikings from Norway and Denmark conquered and then settled in all of England except Wessex. They were defeated by Alfred the Great of Wessex in 886, but were back in control by 1016.

Meanwhile, in 843 the Highland tribes of Picts and Scots were united into one kingdom under King Kenneth MacAlpin. The Lowlands of Scotland were inhabited by Britons and Angles from Northumbria. Wales was mostly settled by Celts by the eighth century, when family groupings became small kingdoms.

The Anglo-Saxons developed communal strip farming using large plows. A council of wise men—the Witan—issued laws and chose kings.

The history of Britain after Roman times is marked by the names of the succeeding royal houses, such as the Normans, Plantagenets, and Tudors.

THE NORMANS

The last great Saxon king, King Edward the Confessor, who reigned from 1042 to 1066, allegedly promised the English throne to Duke William of Normandy, but when Edward died, Harold Godwinson of Wessex became king instead. In 1066 Duke William invaded the south and defeated Harold in the Battle of Hastings and claimed the English throne.

King William I, also known as William the Conqueror, saw England as the Crown's personal property. He deprived most Saxon lords of their lands and gave half to Norman nobles, one quarter to the church, and kept most of what remained for himself. Royal hunting grounds such as the New Forest in Hampshire date from William's time. The *Domesday Book* of 1086 records landholdings and agricultural practices after William's land redistribution.

As Duke of Normandy, William gave nominal allegiance to the king of France. The business of governing Britain was conducted wherever King William and his royal court happened to be, since he traveled constantly.

The Bayeux Tapestry recounts, in more than 60 episodes, the expedition across the English Channel by William the Conqueror and his victory over Harold. In this particular scene, the appearance of Halley's Comet in 1066 is also recorded.

The investiture of Prince Charles as prince of Wales in 1969 when he was 21 years old. The Prince of Wales has been the eldest son of the reigning monarch since 1284. This title will pass to Prince William when Prince Charles, the current prince of Wales, becomes king.

THE PLANTAGENETS

William's death was followed by disputes over the throne. Subsequent monarchs strengthened ties with France by marriage, and even claimed the French throne.

The murder of the archbishop Thomas à Becket in Canterbury Cathedral in 1170 was part of the Church-State dispute during the reign of Henry II (1154–89). Richard I (1189–99), known as Richard the Lionheart, went on several crusades to the Holy Land. His brother, King John, ruled so badly that the nobles forced him to sign the Magna Carta in 1215. The document guaranteed many political rights and personal liberties in Britain. During the reign of Henry III (1216–72), nobles led by Simon de Montfort formed a council that became the parliament. Edward I (1272–1307) conquered Wales, killing the Welsh leader Llewelyn in 1282 and installing his own son, Edward II, as Prince of Wales in Caernarvon Castle in 1284. He also installed his own nominee on the throne of Scotland, but Edward II was defeated by the Scots at the Battle of Bannockburn in 1314 and Scotland remained independent.

Further disputes occurred in the late 14th and early 15th centuries. Edward II (1307–27) was deposed and murdered. Under Edward III (1327–77), England fought the Hundred Years' War with France, which lasted from 1337 to 1453 and resulted in the loss of all English-owned French lands except Calais. This period was also marked by the Black Death, a form of plague spread by rat fleas, that killed up to 45 percent of the population between 1348 and 1350.

Under Henry VI (1422–61), the nobles divided into the houses of Lancaster and York in the Wars of the Roses. When Edward IV (1461–83) died, Richard of Gloucester imprisoned Edward's sons in the Tower of London, where they were murdered, and then declared himself Richard III (1483–85).

THE TUDORS AND EARLY STUARTS

HENRY VII AND VIII Henry Tudor defeated Richard III in 1485 to become Henry VII (1485–1509). Although he was a Lancastrian, he married Elizabeth of York to end the feud. He pacified the powerful Welsh nobles and brought them under his control, and he tried to make the English crown financially independent. His son, Henry VIII (1509–47), involved England in long military campaigns on the European continent. Henry VIII married six times and caused a split between the English Church and the papal authority in Rome. Under him, an Act of Union joined Wales to England in 1536. Wales gained representation in the parliament and place names were changed from Welsh to English.

Caernarvon Castle in northern Wales, the traditional site for the investiture of the prince of Wales since 1284.

EDWARD VI Henry VIII's son, Edward VI (1547–53), ruled as a minor, during which time the Protestant religion was practiced, but under Edward's stepsister Mary (1553–58), Protestant preachers were persecuted, and England reverted to Roman Catholicism.

ELIZABETH I Protestantism returned once more with Elizabeth I (1558–1603). During her reign, considered one of the most glorious, the Spanish Armada was defeated, English colonies were planted in America, and learning and the arts flourished.

Elizabeth I never married, so the throne passed to her cousin James VI of Scotland, who became James I of England (1603–25). His accession cemented the two countries together, although this was only finalized a century later with the Act of Union of 1707. Under James, the Authorized Version of the Bible was published in 1611, and the *Mayflower* set off from Plymouth in 1620 to found a new Puritan colony in America.

THE CIVIL WAR AND THE RESTORATION

Portrait of Elizabeth I.

Both James I and his son Charles I (1625–49) became increasingly dependent on Parliament for money to run the government. Every time Parliament granted further taxes, it demanded new powers. The 1628 Petition of Right, granting individual citizens freedom from arbitrary arrest and imprisonment, is one of the most far-reaching results of this period. Charles I further antagonized Parliament by marrying a Roman Catholic.

He also tried to impose Anglican Church practice on the fiercely Puritan Scottish Kirk (church), which led to war with Scotland.

To fight the Scots, Charles had to ask Parliament for more money. In 1642 his attempt to arrest five Members of Parliament in the House of Commons precipitated a civil war. The war between Royalists and Parliamentarians lasted until 1645, when the Royalists were defeated at the Battle of Naseby. In 1649 Charles I and his wife, Henrietta Maria, were executed, and England became a Commonwealth under Oliver Cromwell until his death in 1658. Sporadic fighting continued against the Royalists.

Reenactment of a battle in the Civil War by the Sealed Knot Society, a historical society that re-enacts important historical battles.

By 1660, with no clear sign of a new leader, Charles II (1660–85), son of the executed monarch, was asked to return from exile to the throne. This period is called the Restoration. The Test Act of 1673 precluded any Catholic from holding public office. Charles II was careful to be accommodating in his reign, but his brother James II (1685–88) tried to overturn anti-Catholic legislation, married a Catholic, and was believed by many to be a Catholic himself.

Highland dress, including the tartan, was forbidden under the Act of Proscription until it was repealed in 1782.

THE GLORIOUS REVOLUTION

Parliament invited the Dutch King William, married to Charles II's daughter Mary, to invade in the name of Protestantism, which he did in 1688 in what became known as the Glorious Revolution. James fled to France. William (1688–1702) and Mary (1688–94) were offered the crown jointly by Parliament. From that time, Parliament was stronger than the crown in Britain. In 1689 a Bill of Rights, which guaranteed individual liberties including the freedom of religion, was passed. In 1701 an Act of Settlement was adopted that allowed only a Protestant to inherit the crown, a law still in force today.

William defeated James II and his Roman Catholic supporters at the Battle of the Boyne in Ireland in 1690. Stuart supporters (called Jacobites) in Scotland rebelled in the early 18th century, which resulted in the Act of Union of 1707 that joined Scotland to England. James II's son James led a Jacobite rebellion in Scotland in 1715. In another rebellion, James II's grandson, Bonnie Prince Charlie, defeated an English army at Edinburgh in 1745 but was eventually defeated in 1746 at the Battle of Culloden.

After William and Mary, the throne passed to Anne (1702–14), Charles II's other daughter, and then to George of Hanover, great grandson of James I.

By 1714 Britain was the leading international power, with 12 colonies on the eastern coast of America, sugar possessions in the West Indies, a flourishing slave trade between Africa and America, and expanding trading interests in India, the Far East, and the Pacific.

Economic life expanded. New canals and waterways improved the distribution of goods, and weekly markets were replaced by regularly stocked shops. Agricultural reforms and the fencing in of land led to widespread rural poverty and a mobile labor force—preconditions for the 19th-century Industrial Revolution.

THE INDUSTRIAL REVOLUTION

An increasing population's demand for clothes, goods, and houses, coupled with growing scientific knowledge and inventions, led to the Industrial Revolution. Instead of doing handwork at home, workers at machines in factories produced large numbers of goods, and Britain became "the workshop of the world."

The textile industry benefited greatly from scientific inventions. James Hargreaves' spinning jenny of the 1760s spun thread on multiple spinning wheels, Richard Arkwright's water frame further refined spinning and harnessed water power successfully, while Samuel Crompton's mule-jenny combined the two. Edmund Cartwright invented a power loom in 1785 that used animal power at first and steam power later.

Abraham Darby's invention of the coke-smelting process in Coalbrookdale in 1709 enabled Britain to use its large natural deposits of iron, while Henry Cort invented a "puddling" process for making wrought or malleable iron, as opposed to cast iron. He also invented a rolling mill. Darby's grandson built the first iron bridge across the Severn at Ironbridge, which opened in 1779 *(below)*. In the 1780s, the first iron ship was built, as were cast-iron pipes for city water systems.

The coal industry also benefited from scientific inventions. In the early 1700s, a steam pump

helped to drain pits. This was refined by James Watt into the steam engine in 1769. Steam power was used for draining and hauling in the coal industry, and further improvements in propping, lighting, and ventilation developed during the 19th century. The steam engine was adopted by other manufacturing industries and formed the basis of Stephenson's Rocket, the first steam locomotive, in 1829 that triggered the mid-19th-century railway boom. Engineering and machine tool industries also developed.

The growth of new industrial towns such as Manchester, with their own merchant classes, led to major social change and growing political demands. Working conditions in factories and coal pits were highly exploitative but were gradually improved during the 19th century. Not everyone welcomed the new machinery. Old hand weavers attacked the new machines; they became known as Luddites after a mythical leader, Ned Ludd, and held protests against technological innovation in northern England in the 19th century.

THE HANOVERIANS

The period from the 18th to the early 19th century, when Britain was ruled by the Hanover monarchs, was marked by significant victories in major wars. Britain was victorious in its war with France (1756–63), where France lost all its territories in North America. Although it lost in the American Revolution (1775–83), Britain's victory over France in the Napoleonic Wars (1793–1815) earned it 20 colonies. By 1820 Britain had colonized a quarter of the world's population, cementing its power and reputation.

THE VICTORIAN AGE Queen Victoria (1837–1901) presided over a golden age of British expansion, imperialism, and world domination. The two-party system in Parliament evolved in the 1860s, as Benjamin Disraeli and William Gladstone alternated as prime ministers and heads of the Conservative and Liberal governments respectively.

Overseas trade led to many foreign entanglements: in 1839, the start of the Opium Wars with China; in 1854, the Crimean War against the Russians; and in 1857, the Indian Mutiny, which briefly cast doubts on the colonial philosophy. Suez in Egypt was invaded in 1882 to protect Britain's shipping route to India. The Boer War (1899–1902) took place in South Africa amidst growing competition with other European powers for African colonies.

THE EARLY 20TH CENTURY

The age of King Edward VII (1902–10) was overshadowed by a growing European military build-up and the onset of World War I in 1914. Huge casualties in trench warfare were suffered at the Battle of the Somme (France) in 1916 and at Passchendaele (Belgium) in 1917. There were over 1 million British casualties in World War I. The suffragette movement for

women's political rights gained momentum in the prewar years. During the war, women took the places of men away at war in armaments factories and agriculture, and at the end of the war in 1918, women over the age of 30 gained the right to vote for the first time.

Home rule had been agreed for Ireland just before the outbreak of the war. A bloody Irish uprising during Easter in 1916 was suppressed harshly by English troops. In 1921 the Anglo-Irish Treaty, which divided the Roman Catholic south from the Protestant north, was signed.

During the 1920s, Britain experienced a severe economic depression and high unemployment. Unrest in the coal industry led to the General Strike of 1926, when workers from all industries stopped working for a week. The world economic crisis hit Britain hard during the 1930s, with the industrial heartlands of South Wales, the Midlands, and the north of England particularly affected. From 1937 onward, the armaments industry revived as Britain prepared for the war against Germany that broke out in 1939. Winston Churchill became a revered and respected wartime prime minister.

Edward VIII abdicated in 1936 to marry American divorcee Wallis Simpson.

POSTWAR BRITAIN

In the 1940s and 1950s, there were food shortages and rationing in Britain, as well as large-scale reconstruction. Social measures passed during these years form the basis of the existing welfare system.

Gradually, Britain's former colonies gained their independence. In 1973 the United Kingdom joined the European Community, now called the European Union (EU). The European Union is a community of 25 nations bound together by common policies on such aspects as trade, environment, agriculture, and education. These policies are created by EU governing institutions. As part of the European Union, Britain has had to adopt EU laws and regulations on many areas of British society, including labor laws, human rights, racial discrimination, and the environment.

Politics developed largely into a Labour-Conservative seesaw. The oil crisis of 1973, where oil supply was cut and prices soared, rocked the economy, and increasing union demands against a backdrop of unemployment brought down the Labour government in 1979.

Radical economic reforms were introduced in Britain by the government led by Margaret Thatcher. They aimed to reduce the role of government so that market conditions could flourish. Thatcher was a successful wartime leader during the Falklands War of 1982 and developed an enduring friendship with U.S. President Ronald Reagan. Her attitude to the increasingly important European Union was less accommodating and was an important factor in her downfall. Thatcher ceded the leadership of the Conservative Party to John Major in 1990. He broadly continued her policies, although he was much more pro-Europe.

NEW LABOUR

In 1997 the Labour Party under Tony Blair swept to power with a staggering majority of 179 seats. An elected mayoralty was established for London, Scotland, and Wales, and each received their own regional assemblies. Reform of the House of Lords began, ending the traditional right of hereditary peers to sit in Parliament. In 1998 the Good Friday Agreement provided for a Northern Ireland Assembly and a power-sharing executive.

Former prime minister Margaret Thatcher, now Lady Thatcher, was one of Britain's most dynamic and controversial leaders. She won three successive elections and held office from 1979 to 1990, when she was ousted from the leadership by her own party in their attempt to gain electoral support.

MARCH FOR
LIBERTY &
LIVELIHOOD
LONDON
22nd SEPT 2002

GOVERNMENT

THE UNITED KINGDOM of Britain, which includes England, Scotland, Wales, and Northern Ireland is a constitutional monarchy. The monarch has a predominantly ceremonial role as head of state, with duties that include the formal appointment of the prime minister, accepting the resignations of prime ministers before elections, and opening Parliament each year. The monarch also meets the prime minister weekly to discuss current issues and receives and entertains foreign heads of state.

NATIONAL GOVERNMENT

The government is a parliamentary democracy. Elections are held at least every five years. All citizens on the electoral roll over the age of 18 can vote, although it is not compulsory to do so. Generally, the political party that wins the most number of seats forms the government.

The day-to-day business of government is decided by a cabinet of up to 21 ministers chosen by the prime minister. The cabinet includes the chancellor of the exchequer—the minister who presents the annual budget on the country's finances—and ministers representing the different government departments, in charge of home affairs, foreign affairs, education, and health, among others.

Above: Some of the buildings in Whitehall, the street in London where Britain's government offices are located.

Opposite: The famous clock tower at the eastern wing of the Houses of Parliament.

PARLIAMENT

The United Kingdom has a two-tier parliamentary system. Bills are debated and passed first in the House of Commons, or lower house, which has 659 elected Members of Parliament (MPs) representing constituencies in England, Wales, Scotland, and Northern Ireland. Each constituency has approximately 60,000 voters.

Proceedings in the House of Commons are chaired by the Speaker, who recognizes MPs in turn and keeps order in the sometimes unruly debates. The prime minister has to face Parliament each week to face questions on the running of the country. Parliamentary debates are televised, reported on the radio, and recorded verbatim in a publication called *Hansard*. Parliamentary committees are formed to investigate policies, with members of different political parties taking part. The Public Accounts Committee, for example, questions the government's spending policies.

The House of Lords, the upper house, debates those bills that have passed the House of Commons, and its role is generally to give assent to their passage. Its members are called peers. Debate is more leisurely and gentlemanly than in the House of Commons. The House of Lords has not historically been a representative body and consists of the Lords Spiritual (the two archbishops and other bishops of the Anglican Church), the Law Lords (those at the head of the legal system), and the Lords Temporal (those appointed based on outstanding deeds, especially in public life, and with a noble or aristocratic background). In 1999 the House of Lords Act was passed, paving the way for reform of the upper house to make it an elected second chamber of Parliament. An independent commission was set up in 2000 for this purpose.

Once bills have passed through both the House of Commons and the House of Lords, the monarch gives Royal Assent to them before they become law.

REGIONAL GOVERNMENT

In 1999 a significant amount of government was transferred from the central government in Westminster to the different regions of the United Kingdom. Called devolution, this decentralization of government was implemented by Blair's Labour government to placate increasing nationalist sentiments, especially in Scotland, and to enable each region to deal with specific needs and circumstances. However, the UK government retains control over foreign policy, defense, and economic and monetary systems, among others.

Scotland now has its own parliament of 129 members in Edinburgh, which can pass laws on education, health, agriculture, transportation, and justice matters, as well as on income tax. Its policies include free long-term personal care for the elderly and no tuition fees for students in higher education.

Wales has its own assembly in Cardiff with 60 elected members. Unlike the Scottish parliament, the Welsh assembly does not have law-making or taxing powers but can develop and implement policies and administer funds throughout the region. Some initiatives that differ from Westminster include free bus travel for senior citizens, extended support for the homeless, and free medical prescriptions for those under 25 years of age.

Both Scotland and Wales also continue to elect members to the UK Parliament in Westminster.

The historic Good Friday Agreement of 1998 provided for a power-sharing devolved government in Northern Ireland. However, the 108-member assembly could not agree over the decommissioning of arms and was suspended in October 2002.

The Channel Islands and the Isle of Man are both self-governing in most aspects of domestic policy.

LOCAL GOVERNMENT

Further radical changes were introduced in Britain's local government structure in the late 1990s. Greater London's 32 boroughs are now overseen by the Greater London Authority, with an elected mayor and London Assembly in overall control of policy. Wales, Scotland, and four former counties of England now have independent authorities, while the remaining 34 counties have both county and smaller, district councils.

POLITICAL PARTIES

While there have always been several political parties represented in Parliament, since World War II the government of Britain has been split between the Conservative Party and the Labour Party. The Conservative Party is committed to encouraging business through lower direct taxes, controlling inflation by limiting government spending, and bringing private enterprise to state-run utilities and infrastructure. By contrast, the Labour Party has historically held socialist values, championing workers' rights, investing to generate employment, and investing heavily in public services. Blair's "new" Labour government of 1997 brought an agenda of low taxes, low spending, and constitutional reforms while keeping many of the previous government's economic reforms. This was a huge step away from traditional Labour policies that favored state ownership of assets and trade union power and allowed Labour to gain the support of businesses.

The Liberal Democratic Party, the third main political party, occupies the central political ground between the Conservative and Labour parties. During the 1970s, the Liberals allied with the Labour Party, and in the 1980s they allied with a new party, the Social Democrats. Initially the new alliance did well in the polls, but unclear direction and disputes between the two groups led to a split and dilution of support. In recent years support for the Liberals has picked up again.

The Green Party, formerly the Ecology Party, enjoys small but growing support for its environmental policies.

REGIONAL POLITICS

WALES Plaid Cymru (Ply-d Kum-ree), the Welsh nationalist party, was founded in 1925 and became active in the 1970s. It has been largely responsible for Wales gaining its own television and radio channels, the reintroduction of the Welsh language into schools in the 1970s, bilingual Welsh and English road signs and government publications, and the demand for devolution that resulted in the Welsh assembly in Cardiff.

SCOTLAND The Scottish National Party also championed Scottish devolution from England and was the official opposition in the first Scottish parliament in Edinburgh. The Scottish National Party and Plaid Cymru want their countries to become full national members of the European Union.

The Central Criminal Court in London, better known as the Old Bailey, is the leading criminal court. The sword and scales represent truth and justice.

NORTHERN IRELAND Two parties, the Ulster Unionists, representing the Protestant cause in Northern Ireland, and the Social Democratic and Labour Party, which is mainly Catholic-oriented, have MPs in the British parliament. Sinn Féin, a nationalist organization that used to be linked with the paramilitary group, the Irish Republican Army, also has elected MPs, but they have refused to take their seats in Parliament. Terrorist activities by extremist groups in Northern Ireland and on the British mainland were regular occurrences in the 1980s and early 1990s. The 1998 Good Friday Agreement aimed to provide peace through a permanent ceasefire.

THE LEGAL SYSTEM

Britain has an uncodified constitution—it is not written in a single document. It relies on a large body of precedent cases, or "common law," that has been built up since the 11th century. In addition to this body of

THE POLICE

Britain has independent police forces corresponding to regional areas, instead of a single national force. There are a total of 147,000 policemen and policewomen, roughly one officer to every 400 citizens. England and Wales have 41 police forces, there are two for London—the Metropolitan Police *(right)* and the City of London Police, and Scotland has another eight units.

The Metropolitan police force of 3,000 constables was established in 1829 by Sir Robert Peel, the home secretary at the time. The nickname "bobby" originated with him.

Other than for specific cases such as antiterrorist work, the police in Britain do not carry firearms, and to do so requires authorization for each particular case.

law, there is legislation passed by Parliament, known as equity law, and law passed by the European Community, which in many cases takes precedence over British domestic law. There are three divisions to the legal system in the United Kingdom: that of England and Wales, that of Scotland, and that of Northern Ireland.

In England and Wales, less serious criminal cases are tried first in magistrates' or local courts. Some large cities also have paid full-time stipendiary magistrates, who sit alone and decide cases. More serious cases are referred to the crown courts. There are 93 of these in England and Wales, each presided over by a judge with a jury of 12 citizens to assess guilt and pass sentences. The Central Criminal Court in London is the ultimate criminal court, while the Royal Courts of Justice is the ultimate civil court. Legal aid, paid for by public funds, is available for victims of crimes and for criminal defendants but is not available for civil cases. The Home Secretary has overall responsibility for the criminal justice system.

In Scotland, most minor criminal cases are tried informally in police courts in the towns and in magistrates' courts in the countryside. More serious criminal cases are tried in the sheriff courts, where the sheriff sits alone for minor cases and with a jury for more serious cases.

Northern Ireland's court system is similar to that of England and Wales.

BRITAIN entered the 21st century with a long period of sustained economic growth, low inflation, low interest rates, and high employment. Gross domestic product (GDP) growth has been more than 3 percent. As a member of the European Union, Britain benefits from a large market for manufactured and agricultural goods. Together with the United States, Japan, Canada, Germany, France, Italy, and Russia, Britain is one of the world's eight leading industrial nations (G8). More than 100 British companies are listed among Europe's top 600 businesses.

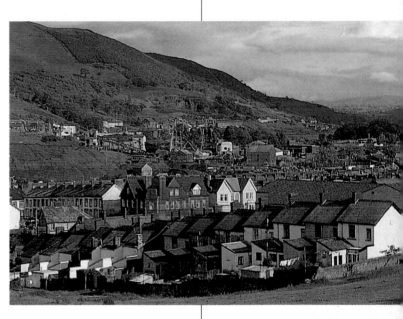

Above: **A mining town in South Wales. Mining communities like this are becoming uncommon due to government closure of mines over the last decade.**

Opposite: **Office workers in Canary Wharf taking a lunch break.**

MANUFACTURING

HEAVY INDUSTRY Britain's heavy manufacturing industry originally developed close to sources of power. For example, heavy engineering, steel production, manufacturing for the oil industry, shipbuilding, and ship repair facilities developed near the Northumberland and Durham coalfields. In nearby Teeside, a chemical industry developed to turn coal by-products, chemicals from the Tees salt field, and oil refinery by-products into paints, fertilizers, explosives, plastics, and textiles. Steel production boomed in South Wales and Sheffield, areas with adjacent coalfields. Manufacturing accounts for one sixth of the British economy, two-thirds of its exports, and 75 percent of business research and development. About 3.5 million people are directly employed in manufacturing, with many more in related supply chains, services, and transportation industries.

Canary Wharf, located in an area of former docks and shipping wharves, was developed in the 1980s as an extension of the financial center of the City of London.

AUTOMOTIVE INDUSTRY Automobiles are a large source of manufactured exports. Car production and sales are at record levels, and Britain is a world leader in the manufacture and technology of race cars.

OTHER SECTORS Britain's aerospace sector is the second largest in the world, employing over 150,000 people. The construction sector generates 10 percent of Britain's GDP and employs 1.4 million, and its output is among the 10 largest in the world. Engineering and electrotechnical industries generated a turnover of £93 billion ($171 billion) in 1999. Britain is the European Union's fifth largest producer of footwear.

Some former industrial areas in the northeast, northwest, and the Midlands are now benefiting from Japanese investment in industrial expansion zones. These zones allow investors to benefit from tax incentives as well as use Britain as a springboard into the EU market.

The corridor beside the M4 freeway linking London to South Wales has attracted high-technology industries. The easy access to markets and airports, and an attractive working environment combined with a pool of highly trained personnel, have led to a booming computer industry. Software businesses currently account for around 3 percent of Britain's GDP.

SOURCES OF ENERGY

The British coal industry is in decline. In July 2004, Britain had 14 working coal pits, soon to be reduced to 11, with more than 6,000 employees. Coal-fired power stations produce greenhouse gases, so power companies are increasingly choosing to use more environmentally friendly sources of energy, such as gas.

In the 1960s, oil was discovered in the North Sea. Profitable fields lie to the east of mainland Scotland near the Orkney Islands. Sullom Voe on the Shetland Islands, Scapa Flow on the Orkney Islands, and Aberdeen on the mainland have all become important oil and gas ports, with oil-fired power stations located nearby. There are now 240 offshore gas fields in production, but output is declining and is expected to continue doing so for the next 20 years. Currently Britain has the largest reserves of oil in the European Union, although oil production is also decreasing. Scotland and part of Northumbria have some hydroelectric power, a result of high rainfall in these areas. In Kinlochleven, Scotland, hydroelectric power is used to smelt aluminum. Nuclear power stations are located in remote coastal areas of Scotland, the northwest, along the southern coast, East Anglia, and the Bristol Channel. Twenty-five percent of Britain's electricity is generated from nuclear power; while much of the rest is from fossil fuels such as coal.

INFRASTRUCTURE

Britain's network of roads extends outward from London to the rest of the country. The major freeways, generally three lanes in each direction, suffer frequent traffic jams.

Passenger rail fares are among the most expensive in Europe. Trains on different sections of the rail network are run by private rail companies, with a separate company controlling the track throughout Britain. The Channel Tunnel opened in 1994, providing a 31-mile (50-km) rail link from Folkestone, England, to Calais, France.

Traffic congestion is a frequent occurrence in the major cities. Inner-city traffic congestion is a growing problem.

The London Underground system has 254 miles (410 km) of railway track. At peak hours, trains are frequently overcrowded. Buses are a crucial component of the public transportation system.

Seventy-seven percent of Britain's trade is carried by sea from 300 ports. Now that the country's trade is predominantly with the European Union, Channel ports, such as Dover, and those on the eastern coast, such as Felixstowe, have become more important.

THE SERVICE SECTOR

Retailing is Britain's top service industry, employing 3 million people or 11 percent of the workforce. Much of the retail market is controlled by the large stores and chains. Laws that allow supermarkets to open for a maximum of six hours on Sundays are meant to help smaller businesses compete.

The National Health Service, the main provider of healthcare in Britain, is the third largest employer in the world, with its 1.5 million employees. It manages an annual budget of £40 billion ($74 billion), the administration of which is often controversial.

Medical systems and pharmaceuticals are other important businesses in this sector. Britain supplies a quarter of the world market's single-use disposable products. In addition, business services, insurance, marketing and advertising, market research, conference and exhibition organization, and management consultancy are all growth areas.

FINANCE AND BANKING

Britain's leading international financial services center employs 1 million people and generates 5.1 percent of Britain's GDP. The country has the highest concentration of foreign banks in the world; in 2000 there were 481 such banks. The London Stock Exchange is a major trading center. Eurobonds, stocks, and funds are all traded in London and Manchester. The City of London is the historic financial center, although many leading institutions now have offices in Canary Wharf.

The Bank of England in central London.

The Bank of England is the government's banker and prints bank notes. Since 1997 it has been free to set monetary policy by deciding short-term interest rates. This has improved economic stability and growth.

In 2003 Britain's public debt was the lowest of any G8 country.

ENVIRONMENT

BRITAIN'S ENVIRONMENTAL CONCERNS are similar to those faced by most industrialized countries. A dense population and high energy use for commercial and household purposes, transportation, and housing produces large amounts of waste. Advocacy groups such as Greenpeace and Friends of the Earth have raised awareness of environmental concerns, which are now major issues for the political parties. The government has set very ambitious targets for a number of environmental matters, in spite of the fact that many concerns are global in nature.

The main agencies responsible for environmental protection in Britain—the Department for the Environment, Food, and Rural Affairs (DEFRA) and the Environment Agency—work closely together.

AIR POLLUTION

Vehicles are the greatest source of carbon dioxide emissions in Britain. In 1970 there were under 10 million private cars; by 2002 the figure was over 24 million. Virtually all private cars now run on unleaded gasoline, and sulphur emissions from diesel-fueled cars are being reduced. Local councils attempt to regulate traffic congestion through park-and-ride schemes on the outskirts of busy towns and through parking restrictions within residential areas.

Other sources of pollution include power stations, which produce 70 percent of Britain's sulphur dioxide emissions, and large landfills, which contribute methane.

Above: **Filtering in power stations has reduced sulphur dioxide emissions.**

Opposite: **A valley in the county of Clwyd in north-eastern Wales.**

A traffic jam in London.

TRAFFIC WOES

THE LONDON CONGESTION CHARGE In February 2003 the mayor of London, Ken Livingstone, introduced a congestion charge of £5 ($9) a day on all vehicles entering an area of central London between 7:00 A.M. and 6:30 P.M. on weekdays. This has significantly reduced the number of vehicles and hence journey times within the zone. Congestion has been reduced by an average of 30 percent, and buses now travel faster and more frequently within the area as a result.

A western extension to the zone is under consideration, and if it goes ahead it is expected to take effect in 2006 or later.

THE WALKING BUS Several local councils and schools are working to reduce the number of cars bringing children to and from school. School buses are not common in Britain, so children are encouraged to walk in supervised groups called walking buses. This program also helps reduce childhood obesity by requiring more exercise of children.

WATER POLLUTION

Britain has made great progress in cleaning up its inland and coastal waterways: rivers, canals, and beaches. Nearly 99 percent of England's beaches comply with European bathing quality standards, and in 2004 a total of 118 beaches in the United Kingdom were given Blue Flag awards for excellence in cleanliness, safety, water quality, and facilities.

At various times there have been oil spills off the coasts that have caused great damage to marine life, and the impact takes a while to dissipate. DEFRA has guidelines on using dispersants to minimize damage to the marine environment.

Criooieth in Wales, one of the Blue Flag beaches.

ENERGY AND THE ENVIRONMENT

Britain's energy is derived predominantly from fossil fuels. Coal, oil, and natural gas are all used in power stations to produce electricity. Rigorous emissions standards and regulations are enforced, in compliance with national and EU laws and international guidelines. Britain's nuclear power industry supplies around 25 percent of the country's electricity. However, no new nuclear power stations are being commissioned, so when the current 16 stations reach the end of their working lives there will be an energy shortfall.

More environmentally friendly sources of energy include wind farms, river dams, and combined heat and power (CHP), where the heat generated in the production of electricity is also used. Renewable energy was 1 percent of Britain's energy output in 2002. The government hopes to increase this to 10 percent by 2010.

WIND FARMS

Britain is increasing the number of wind farms to produce electricity in an environmentally friendly manner. A typical wind farm covers roughly 0.4 square miles (1 square km) of land and holds about 20 wind turbines. Wind farms are located on high ground and in areas of sparse population, such as Cornwall, Cumbria, Wales, Yorkshire, Northern Ireland, and Scotland. Winds of between 10 and 33 miles per hour (16 and 53 km per hour) are ideal for effective turbine use: with stronger winds, the turbines will shut down to prevent damage. A 600-kw turbine can produce enough electricity for 375 households.

Farmers generally do not mind wind farms, since they can continue to use most of the land around the turbines either for growing crops or raising livestock. But there are people who object to wind farms. Often they live nearby and find the turbines unsightly. Others find fault with the noise from the rotating blades. Fears that the rotating blades may frighten sheep and other animals have proved unfounded. The first British wind farm in Delabole, Cornwall, has a stud farm and riding stable in the area.

Offshore wind farms are slightly more expensive to build, but they get stronger and more constant winds and thus generate more electricity. Blyth Harbour in Northumberland and North Hoyle in Wales are home to offshore wind farms.

About 20 new wind farm projects, both on land and offshore, were underway in 2004, with the goal of using wind power to generate 1.3 percent of Britain's electricity by 2005.

CLIMATE CHANGE

Britain is a major supporter of the Kyoto Protocol, an agreement among industrialized nations to reduce greenhouse-gas emissions, and is implementing measures to reduce further damage to the ozone layer and thus slow down global warming. The country is also a key member of the Intergovernmental Panel on Climate Change.

Climate change affects all aspects of the environment. Up to 10 percent of Britain's total land area, inhabited by 6 million people, is a flood plain, and flooding has become more frequent. At the current rate of climate change, London's flood defenses will need to be redesigned or replaced by 2030. In addition, coastal erosion threatens significant parts of the eastern coasts.

There are more than 2,000 landfill sites in Britain. About a quarter of the total waste in the country is sent to landfill sites.

WASTE DISPOSAL

Over 400 million tons of waste is produced annually in Britain, of this, 29 million tons comes from households. Only 12 percent of household and 40 percent of industrial and commercial waste is recycled, among the lowest rates in Europe. Britain hopes to recycle 25 percent of household waste. Recycling containers are available in all towns and supermarkets. Many urban councils collect sorted recycleable waste, such as glass, cans, newspapers, and cardboard.

EU legislation strictly controls the disposal of electrical and electronic equipment. All refrigerators and freezers in stores now minimize chlorofluorocarbon (CFC) use. The Environment Agency gives free advice to companies to improve environmental efficiency and save money.

The population of sparrows, once one of Britain's most common birds, has decreased from 25 million in the 1970s to about 13 million now. This could be because of changing farming practices and locked cereal feeders.

Opposite: **Twelve species of whale and dolphin live in British coastal waters.**

WILDLIFE CONSERVATION

A system of national parks, conservation areas, places of outstanding natural beauty, and green belts near cities ensure a balance between the immediate needs of Britain's people and the protection of wildlife and natural habitats. Changing agricultural practices have reduced the number of hedgerows in some areas, while nitrate fertilizers increase crop yield at the expense of birds and small mammals. Lowland heaths, traditional grasslands, and salt marshes are all declining.

There is a mixed picture of decline and recovery for Britain's wildlife. Between 10 and 20 percent of indigenous species of freshwater fish, nonmarine reptiles and amphibians, and seed plants are endangered. Approximately 220 different species of birds nest in Britain, of which 139 species are in decline; 23 have declined by half in the past 25 years. The red squirrel population is now down to only 30,000, concentrated in a few select areas such as the Isle of Wight, Cumbria, and Northumberland. Both seal and otter populations have come back from dangerously low levels. Bats are well protected by law, as are owls. Urban foxes are thriving in very different environments from their original habitats.

Over 70 percent of Britain's fish stocks are either fully or over-exploited. Fish stocks are regulated by internationally agreed fishing quotas, and bad fishing practices such as the use of drift nets, which catch dolphins and other sea mammals unintentionally, have been stopped. Britain is a leading member of the International Whaling Commission and is strongly opposed to any kind of whaling.

DEFRA aims to preserve Britain's marine biodiversity, safeguarding over 44,000 marine species through measures such as protecting cold coral habitats and encouraging sustainable development and coastal management. Angling, fishing in rivers and reservoirs, is the most popular sport in

England and Wales— more people participate in it than in soccer.

There is a tradition of local popular protest against road expansion, housing development, and other activities that deplete the country's natural heritage. A highway was built in the West Country with a tunnel for hedgehogs to cross safely, while protesters have from time to time chained themselves to trees to try to prevent the construction of bypasses.

The UK Biodiversity Action Plan was implemented in 1994, with programs to protect species and habitats and promote public awareness on biodiversity issues.

ORGANIC FOOD

Consumers increasingly choose to buy marginally more expensive organic farm produce; this includes crops produced without chemicals or fertilizers, and animals reared naturally and humanely. There is huge consumer resistance to the introduction of genetically modified crops, largely for fear of the damage that they may cause to the environment. Prince Charles is a vocal advocate of organic farming; his estate in Gloucestershire is organic and produces a range of breads, biscuits, and other goods for sale.

THE BRITISH

PEOPLE IN BRITAIN would generally consider themselves Welsh, Scottish, Irish, English, West Indian, or Bangladeshi rather than British. Local or regional loyalties often supercede national ones. The population is immensely varied, especially in the urban areas of Greater London and the West Midlands. Close to 4 million people in Britain, or roughly 7 percent of the country's population, belong to a minority ethnic group.

THE EARLIEST SETTLERS

Britain, like the United States, has a long and proud history of immigration. Some of the people living in Cornwall, Wales, and western Scotland can trace their ancestry back to the Celtic tribes that populated these areas more than 10 centuries ago.

Angles, Saxons, and Vikings all left their mark in a basic Celto-Roman gene pool, augmented by the invading Normans in 1066. Migrations throughout the European continent over the centuries also added to the British mixture. The migrants included weavers from Flanders, Huguenots (Protestants) who were expelled from France by Louis XIV, refugees fleeing from continental wars during the 16th and 17th centuries, and French nobles fleeing the extremes of the French Revolution in the 18th century.

Above and opposite: **Some of the many different faces of the British.**

DRESS

The British dress similarly to people in other Western nations. The cold, damp winters require heavy coats or mackintoshes (also known as raincoats), warm woolens, and occasionally even long johns—long woolen underwear. When the sun comes out, the British quest for a suntan begins. People sunbathe on beaches, in their own gardens, and in public parks.

One of the best-known local traditional dress variations is the Scottish tartan. This fabric with a plaid design is traditionally made into a kilt. Each Scottish clan has its own tartan, and only those with ancestral links to a clan should wear its tartan.

A man's full Highland dress includes kilts made of pleated woolen tartan held together with a large safety pin, a sporran, or ornamental pouch, over the kilt, a tweed jacket, a flat cap with a central pompon (only worn outdoors), and long socks with a knife inside one sock. In Highland dress, the women wear long tartan skirts, white blouses, and tartan sashes.

Examples of Welsh national dress can be seen at the annual arts festivals and regional variations at local summer shows.

The word tartan first appeared in the 15th century, but the Romans referred to their enemies, the Caledonians [Scots], as "wearing chequered garments."

IMMIGRANT RACES

Britain's Jewish community dates to the 11th century. Many major merchant banks and stockbrokerage houses were founded by Jewish families. Numerous patrons of the arts, theater producers, politicians, and community leaders in Britain also come from the Jewish community. Jews came from Central Europe, Hungary, Poland, and Russia in the 19th century, and from Nazi Germany in the 20th century. One third of all British Jews now live in northwestern London, with a sixth of the total Jewish population living in the London borough of Barnet.

Britain enticed laborers from its colonies to help in the postwar reconstruction at home. The S.S. Empire Windrush carried the first skilled and semiskilled West Indian workers in 1948. Immigration from the Caribbean colonies increased from 11,000 in 1954 to 34,000 in 1962, after the United States introduced immigration controls in the early 1950s.

The majority of Britain's West Indian population settled in Greater London. Thousands of Asian immigrants from India, Pakistan, and Bangladesh arrived in the 1950s, settling in Greater London and in manufacturing towns with acute labor shortages. Ugandan president Idi Amin's expulsion of Asians in 1972 drove 27,000 highly trained and talented Asians of Pakistani descent to Britain.

Approximately 300,000 Chinese, mainly from Hong Kong, have also set up small businesses and entered professions in Britain. London has a Chinatown, and most towns throughout England now have Chinese take-out restaurants. Vietnamese boat people fleeing their Communist government were initially accepted in the early 1980s, but immigration controls have since tightened. Immigration increased in the 1990s from Eastern Europe and the Balkans, especially during the conflicts in Bosnia and Kosovo.

With 950 people per square mile (380 per square km), England is the second most densely populated country in Europe after the Netherlands. Immigration and nationality acts now make it hard to migrate to Britain, and complex procedures exist for those claiming asylum.

Many South Asian immigrants own general stores in Britain's towns and cities.

ENGLISH SURNAMES

Many British surnames originated several centuries ago and often give clues about early ancestors—where they came from, who they were related to, and so on. Here are some examples.

- Names of nearby places, generally towns—London, Ashby, Baldock. Some French place names appear as surnames—Beecham (Beauchamps), Manners (Meunières). Fleming (from Flanders), and Bremner (from Brabant) also reflect places of origin.
- Names of landscape features—Hill, Brooks, Bridges. Surnames such as Atlee, Townsend, Noakes, and Nash form part of this group, as they combine prepositions (at, end) with the geographical feature.
- Personal names—Peter, William, Donald—and their sons—Peterson, Williamson, and Donaldson. In Scotland the prepositions Fitz and Mac mean "son of," as in FitzWilliam, and MacIntosh. Fitz has also been used as a surname for illegitimate royal children—Fitzroy, with Roy being a rendering of the French word *roi* meaning king. In Wales "Ap" shortened to "P" also means "son of"—Prichard (son of Richard), Pugh (son of Hugh), and Powell (son of Howell).
- Names of occupations, trades, offices, or status—Cooper, Weaver, King, Bishop. Regional variations for the same occupation occur, so that the surnames Tucker, Fuller, and Walker are all surnames from the same process of fulling, or cleaning cloth.
- Names from nicknames, expressions, and animals—Long, Black, Cruikshank (crooked leg), Goodenough, Gough (red-haired), Fox, Herring.
- Relationships—Cousins, Fodder, Vaughan (younger).

RACIAL DISCRIMINATION AND INTEGRATION

There are strict laws regarding employment and civil equality in Britain. It is illegal to advertise job vacancies on the basis of color, creed, or sex, and the Commission for Racial Equality can take employers to court for discriminatory practices. The Race Relations (Amendment) Act of 2000 requires that major public bodies promote racial equality. In 2004, 12 out of 659 members of Parliament came from ethnic minorities.

Helping the police. Efforts are being made to improve race relations between the police and minority communities.

Intolerance of immigrants and support for extremist right-wing organizations has been strongest in the poorer inner-city areas. Immigration and customs officials and police officers seem to detain a disproportionate number of nonwhite people for questioning, and a few notorious civil cases have shown alarming prejudice among some police forces. Tensions and unrest have occasionally boiled over. In the early 1980s, arrests in black, inner-city ghettoes sparked off riots by disaffected youths in Liverpool, Manchester, and southern London. In the summer of 2001, race riots erupted in the northern towns of Oldham, Bradford, and Burnley between Asian and white youths. In Britain, as elsewhere, members of the Muslim community feel alienated in the aftermath of the September 11 attacks in the United States, the wars in Afghanistan and Iraq, and the global war on terror.

The cheapest housing, provided by local councils, is often run down and unpleasant to live in. Graffiti and vandalism are frequent in common areas such as hallways and entrance halls.

CLASS DIVISIONS

Distinctions of accent, topics of conversation and terms used, upbringing, table manners, dress, general deportment, meal times, and preferences for food, drink, and entertainment—all these are clues by which one British person could traditionally size up another's class and place in society.

At the top of the ladder, apart from the monarchy, is the aristocracy. They have dwindling economic power but enjoy tremendous vestigial influence and respect. Five royal dukes, 24 other dukes, 35 marquesses, 204 earls, and 127 viscounts and barons head a list of about 900 hereditary peers and 1,200 baronets. All pass titles and landed estates to their children when they die. A paternalistic outlook, a sense of guardianship of property, and a duty to perform public service are widespread attributes of this class. Twice a year, life peers are created by the monarch from all walks of life, in recognition of their contribution to their field or profession.

The middle classes aspire to move up the social ladder. There are numerous subtle gradations within the middle class. The upper middle classes may have earned money in the professions, but the majority generally inherited sufficient wealth to have benefited from the best education, and they aspire to the aristocratic lifestyle by investing in land. The higher echelons of political and economic power and all walks of public life are still dominated by those who attended one of Britain's exclusive public schools—Eton in particular—and either Oxford or Cambridge University. It is then not surprising that many members of the middle class strive to provide educational advantages for their own children. However, old divisions and categories are being eroded, and new

Cliveden House in Buckinghamshire. Stately homes situated on estates of farmland were the traditional homes of the landed aristocracy. Now, very few can afford the upkeep and taxes. Many of these homes are now open to the public as museums, or have been converted into schools or sanitariums.

ones are taking their place. Sports heroes, television celebrities, and other high-profile personalities, whose wealth and fame far outreach that of most aristocrats, are now increasingly seen as the top tier of society. Inheritance taxes, high labor costs, and falling markets for agricultural products have hit members of the aristocracy hard. The middle class is no longer certain of keeping a job for life, while ensuring a good future for their children through education seems threatened by government initiatives to limit applications from private schools. In 1911 three quarters of the population of Britain were manual workers; by 1991 this had dropped to just over one third.

At the start of the 21st century Britain's unemployment exceeded 4 percent, with a total of 1.4 million looking for work and 876,000 claiming unemployment benefit payments. The consumer spending boom, encouraged by low interest rates and high property prices, had passed this group by. High employment, high taxes, and benefit changes have helped to reduce poverty, but the divisions within society between the richest and the poorest remain enormous.

LIFESTYLE

ECONOMIC CONSIDERATIONS largely determine the lifestyles of different British people. Those who work in well-paid jobs can afford better homes, education, and leisure pursuits. There are great differences between urban and rural lifestyles, as there are between the different regions of the country and the different ethnic communities.

In general, the British have small nuclear families. Similar to other industrialized countries, the birth rate in Britain is declining. Many aspects of British life are similar to those in other Western countries.

Above: **A family outing at a local agricultural fair.**

Opposite: **People enjoying a picnic before the start of a show at an open-air theater.**

FAMILY LIFE

The majority of families have married parents, although an increasing number of people are cohabiting and raising children out of wedlock. Seventy-three percent of parents with children in 2002 were married or cohabiting; the remaining 27 percent were single parents. Social commentators argue that children born to married parents generally benefit from more financial and emotional stability than other children. Britain has the highest rate of teenage pregnancy in Europe, with 39,286 pregnancies in 2002. An educational program in schools is underway in an attempt to reduce this number.

A mother and her children taking a walk in the woods. It is becoming hard to define a typical family with Britain's varied population.

IMMIGRANT COMMUNITIES Family size and structure varies between the different immigrant communities. The West Indian community has a comparatively high proportion of single parents, and marriage often occurs after the children are born. The South Asian population of over 2 million, half of which were born in Britain, has traditionally conservative family structures and large kinship networks of support. Often the family is an economic unit, as exemplified by the numerous small grocery stores or restaurants run by Asians. The small Chinese community is self-reliant, also with a generally conservative family structure.

DIVORCE The divorce rate in Britain is high. Approximately one in three marriages end in divorce. It is possible to divorce for a number of legal reasons, including separation for a period of time.

WOMEN IN THE WORKFORCE In urban areas it is common for both parents to work once the children are in school. Childcare is costly and often difficult to arrange, although whenever possible many families ask

MARRIAGE

Both parties must be over 16 years old to marry. If they are under 18, they need parental consent (except in Scotland). Every town has a registry office, and two witnesses have to be at the ceremony.

Many people marry in religious ceremonies. The Church of England has the authority to solemnize marriages. Members of other denominations and religions are required to have a state registrar present or else they have to marry in a registry office before the ceremony.

nearby relatives and grandparents to help. Women make up nearly half of the national workforce. A working woman's average hourly wage is approximately 82 percent of the working man's. Flexible part-time work and working from home are other options for many families. Fathers are increasingly sharing the wife's domestic duties.

Having parties is a typical way of celebrating children's birthdays. Games and birthday cakes are a must.

CHILDHOOD

Most babies are born in hospitals or birth centers run by midwives. Childcare remains predominantly the woman's concern, but there are some men who stay home to take care of the children while their wives work.

Most children celebrate birthdays, sometimes with afternoon parties and games and a cake. British restaurants, pubs, concert halls, museums, and other public facilities generally welcome children with specially designed meals and activities.

Adolescents often express a certain discontent through a youth culture of music, dress styles, and language. Young people with time on their hands often congregate in public places such as shopping centers and public parks, or join youth clubs and use leisure facilities when they can afford to do so. They often want or need some financial independence from their parents.

EDUCATION

Education is free and compulsory for all children between the ages of 5 and 16.

ENGLAND AND WALES In England and Wales, schools are divided into primary (ages 5–11) and secondary (ages 11–16) schools, with a national curriculum having achievement tests at the ages of 7, 11, 14, and 16. The

major examinations are the General Certificate of Secondary Education (GCSE) taken at age 15 or 16, and the Advanced (A) Level exam at age 17 or 18. Some schools now offer the International Baccalaureate qualification instead of A levels. Nursery schools, run by local education authorities or private foundations, teach those below the age of 5 or 6. A government grant toward the cost of nursery education is available for all 3- to 4-year-olds who go to a private provider rather than a state-funded one.

In addition to state schools, there are privately run, fee-paying schools (known as independent or public schools), where pupils benefit from small classes and a competitive system geared toward university entrance. These schools often have more funds than state schools for extracurricular activities such as sports, drama, and music. Over 600,000 children in the United Kingdom are educated in independent schools.

Some religious groups also run schools, with an emphasis on their faith's values and teachings.

Many children attend nursery school where they are introduced to writing, reading, and drawing. Nursery schools also help children to develop their social skills.

Graduation day at Cambridge University.

SCOTLAND In Scotland, children take the Scottish Certificate of Education at age 15 or 16, which is equivalent to the English GCSE. A year later they take the Higher Education examinations, and after that they can take the Sixth Year Studies exams, equivalent to England's A levels.

HIGHER EDUCATION The A level examinations or their equivalent are needed to enter a university in Britain. University students do not pay tuition fees. The government is trying to encourage more students to attend university, although it is hard for graduates to find suitable employment. There were 300,000 graduates in 2004, but only 80,000 jobs that required graduate qualifications were available.

Polytechnics offer more technical courses and prepare adult students for academic examinations, while more specialized colleges such as the Royal College of Art provide expert instruction to pupils.

OLD AGE

Britain has an aging population. The 2001 census showed 1.1 million people over the age of 85 living in England and Wales, and a population with more people over 60 years old than under 16. Many families move away from grandparents for work reasons, and many old people live in retirement homes.

Pensions are often insufficient to pay for proper food and heat in winter, leading to high winter casualty rates. For old people who own their homes the rise in value of the house is of no benefit as they end up being taxed more heavily on their property. This has led to protests.

Two elderly women enjoying a walk in Green Park in central London.

HEALTHCARE

Basic healthcare is provided free of charge by the National Health Service, funded with tax revenues by the central government. The service, with its rising costs and rising expectations, is a constant subject of political debate.

Doctors' offices are found in all local communities. If a person is very sick, a doctor will make a house call. There is approximately one doctor for every 2,000 persons.

Patients are referred to hospitals by doctors, although there is a shortage of hospital beds. Junior doctors and nurses in hospitals often work extremely long hours, as many senior medical staff prefer to be in private practice.

SOCIAL WELFARE

There are a number of welfare benefits available to the most needy members of the community. The benefits are funded partly by the state, partly by employers, and partly by an indirect tax called national insurance that is paid by employees and the self-employed. Sickness benefits, unemployment benefits, state pensions, widows' pensions, and maternity pay are all funded this way. Income Support is a scheme that covers basic living costs, medical prescriptions, dental care, and school meals. Families earning low incomes can get child or working tax credit. Housing Benefit covers the cost of basic rented housing, while Child Benefit is payable to all mothers, regardless of income, until their children reach the age of 18 or 19. Many welfare payments are collected in person at the nearest post office.

Social security payments account for almost one third of all government expenditure. With an increase in the number of people retiring each year, the amount is set to escalate.

HOUSING

Pensioners line up outside the post office on pension collection day.

There is a wide range of housing types in Britain, from idyllic cottages in the countryside to apartments in the cities. Over 80 percent of Britain's population live in terraced, detached, or semidetached houses or bungalows, while the remainder live in apartments. Of Britain's 25 million domestic dwellings, 17 million were owner-occupied in the 2001 census, and 8 million were rented out. During the 1980s, people were encouraged to buy

74

their own homes, and between 1981 and 2001 owner occupation increased by 40 percent. Ownership was financed by mortgages, but in the early 1990s, a number of homes were repossessed by the savings and loan societies and mortgage companies as interest rates increased, the recession deepened, and people lost their jobs.

Some of the most reasonably priced rental housing used to be provided by local councils to the most needy in their areas. The 1980 Housing Act, which allowed council tenants to buy their council properties, had a devastating effect on housing stock. Public sector housing that is meant for the least wealthy people has declined from 30 percent to 17 percent of all homes. Rising house prices in desirable areas make it hard for those on low incomes, such as nurses and teachers, to live in those areas.

A distressing consequence of the high cost of housing, evident to any visitor to London or other major cities, is the number of homeless people living on the streets, often with only a cardboard box for shelter.

An increasing number of people are becoming homeless and living on the streets, particularly in the larger cities.

RELIGION

BRITAIN is officially a Christian country, although less than 20 percent of the population regularly attend church. Many more attend church only on special occasions such as Christmas, weddings, or funerals. The 2001 census included an optional question on religion, which showed that 71.6 percent of the population of the United Kingdom regarded themselves as Christian. A non-denominational act of collective Christian worship takes place in all schools in England and Wales by law, although pupils of different faiths may absent themselves from this, and the nature of this practice varies greatly across the country. In a similar vein, the British Broadcasting Corporation's (BBC) Radio 4 carries a two-minute program called *Thought for the Day* within its weekday morning news program, featuring speakers of many different faiths raising matters of a spiritual or moral dimension.

Above: **Many people attend church services at Christmas.**

Opposite: **A vicar recites prayers at a service.**

CHRISTIANITY

Many different denominations of Christianity are found in Britain, all with their own adherents. England and Scotland each has its own official church. In Wales, there is an autonomous Anglican church with six dioceses under a single province.

A man, not part of the mainstream Christian churches, advocates his beliefs on the street.

WALES There is an autonomous Anglican church with six dioceses under a single province, with about 120,000 members. The bulk of Welsh Christians are Nonconformist or Methodist, followers of the 18th-century evangelist, John Wesley. His message of hard work and thrift appealed to the growing working classes of the time. The Presbyterian Church of Wales, founded in 1735, has 1,200 chapels, 180 ministries, and 75,000 members.

OTHER PROTESTANT SECTS The Methodist community in Britain is not confined to Wales. A total of 450,000 adult members and a community of 1.3 million is spread across Britain, concentrated predominantly in the old industrial working-class areas. It is one of what are known as the Free Churches, those which reject episcopal rule and hierarchical structures, concentrating instead on local leadership. The strictest Methodists abstain from all alcohol.

Other sects include the Baptists—167,000 people are registered as belonging to the Baptist Unions. The United Reformed Church, with 136,000 registered members, is a melding of the Congregational Church of England and Wales and the Presbyterian Church of England. The Religious Society of Friends, or Quakers, is known for its pacifist views and has 18,000 registered adherents. Smaller sects include the Unitarians, Jehovah's Witnesses, Seventh Day Adventists, Christian Scientists, Spiritualists, and the Salvation

Army, which is best known for its brass bands playing carols and anthems in order to raise money for projects for the poor and destitute.

ROMAN CATHOLICISM There are roughly 5 million Roman Catholics in Britain, of whom 2.2 million are active. The Cardinal Archbishop of Westminster is the senior prelate, and the senior lay Catholic is the Duke of Norfolk. Britain has seven Catholic provinces: four in England, one in Wales, and two in Scotland, each with an archbishop, and below them are 30 dioceses and 3,000 parishes. There are large Catholic communities in Liverpool and Glasgow, cities with large Irish immigrant communities. Elsewhere, local pockets of Catholicism sometimes date back to the days of persecution in the 16th century.

Historically, Catholics have been seen as politically suspect, owing allegiance to the pope in Rome as opposed to the monarch of England. There were Catholic plots against Elizabeth I and James I, and Catholic support for Bonnie Prince Charlie in the 18th century. Even at the start of the 21st century, it would not be possible for a monarch or heir to the throne to marry a Roman Catholic without a major constitutional change.

Jehovah's Witnesses going from door to door.

Muslims at prayer in Southall, London, during the fasting month of Ramadan.

OTHER RELIGIONS

ISLAM Britain's approximately 1.5 million Muslims make up the second largest religious group (2.7 percent in 2001) after Christianity. Pakistani immigrant communities in urban areas in the Midlands, northwest, and London have built mosques and religious organizations. Bradford, a Yorkshire textile town, has a large Muslim community. It was in Bradford that protests against Salman Rushdie's novel *The Satanic Verses* reached an explosive peak in 1989. Bradford also has a Muslim "parliament" (with no constitutional rights or powers) to help Muslims gain a political voice.

British awareness of Islamic needs has increased, and funds are now available and laws in place to allow the setting up of Islamic schools. While the Muslim community is predominantly Pakistani, there are also Muslims from Bangladesh, India, Cyprus, and Saudi Arabia. Some radical Islamic leaders fueled discontent over the war in Iraq, though many Islamic leaders tend to cooperate fully with antiterrorist measures.

RASTAFARIANS

A large number of the Afro-Caribbean community are Rastafarians, recognizable by the green, yellow, and red colors often worn on tams, or hats, and their long dreadlocks.

Ras Tafari was the son of Ras Makonnen of Harar. He became Emperor Haile Selassie of Ethiopia in 1930, at a time when Ethiopia was the only truly independent black country in Africa. Deposed by a military coup led by General Teferi Benti in 1974, Selassie died in jail on August 26, 1975.

Identifying Selassie as the Conquering Lion of Judah and the King of Kings from the Bible's Book of Revelation 19:11 and 16, his followers started a movement in Jamaica in the 1930s and 1940s. This became popular in Britain during the 1970s, as some black communities rejected the Christian idea of accepting suffering in this life because of rewards in the next. They focused instead on the new religion that stressed black identity and the idea of African redemption. The Rastafarian view that the drug marijuana is the "sacred weed" also referred to in the Bible leads them to numerous confrontations with the police.

JUDAISM Britain's Jewish community has roughly 270,000 members, formed into 300 congregations in local synagogues. There are both Sephardim (from Spain, Portugal, and North Africa) and Ashkenazim (from Germany and central Europe). The Ashkenazim are the most numerous. The majority are Orthodox Jews, and their chief spokesman is the Chief Rabbi, while the minority are Reform Jews. Jewish religious practice in Britain has declined over the last 20 years. Roughly one in three Jewish children attend Jewish denominational schools.

Reciting from the Torah, the Jewish holy book, is an important part of the Jewish upbringing.

OTHER RELIGIONS Chinese communities in London and other big cities mainly practice Buddhism. There is also a Sikh community of roughly 300,000 and a Hindu community of over 500,000. There are also Bagwan monks, often dressed in red, orange, or purple, and followers of Hare Krishna, dressed in orange.

A number of people, especially those in urban communities, do not subscribe to a particular faith and classify themselves as atheist, agnostic, or humanist.

LANGUAGE

THE ENGLISH LANGUAGE is the second most widely spoken mother tongue in the world with approximately 377 million speakers. English is the principal language in the United Kingdom, the Republic of Ireland, the United States, Canada, Australia, New Zealand, the Bahamas, Jamaica, Grenada, Trinidad and Tobago, and Guyana. It is also the official language of several African countries, and is used widely as a language of commerce throughout the world.

The pronunciation, usage, vocabulary, and syntax used in different English-speaking countries vary greatly. Just like any other language, English is constantly changing and developing. There are new words for new concepts being added and words falling into disuse or taking different meanings as circumstances change.

Above and opposite: **There are dozens of magazines, newspapers, and tabloids in Britain, such as** *The Times*, *Daily Telegraph*, *The Observer*, *The Sun*, **and** *Daily Mirror*.

THE DEVELOPMENT OF THE ENGLISH LANGUAGE

When the Romans invaded Britain in A.D. 43, the indigenous people spoke the Celtic language, then one of the most widely spoken languages in Europe. Under the Romans, Latin was spoken by the administrators and upper classes, but it did not filter down to the common people.

The English language was brought to Britain by invading Germanic groups from the fifth century onward, who progressively settled the low-lying areas and pushed the Celts to the outlying mountainous areas of Wales and Cornwall. The word English comes from one of these peoples, the Angles, who came from what is now Denmark.

OLD ENGLISH

The language used in Britain between A.D. 450 and 1150 is referred to as Old English. Four different kingdoms existed from the fifth to the eighth centuries—Northumbria, Mercia, Kent, and West Saxony (Wessex)—each with their own language variations. By the 10th century, the West Saxon language became the official language, and most Old English manuscripts were transcribed in that area of the country. *Beowulf*, a 3,000-line epic poem, is the greatest surviving example of the literature and language of this period.

Like other Germanic languages, Old English nouns had cases and genders. The language was originally written in a series of straight lines called runes, which were easy to inscribe on stone or wood. Christian missionaries who arrived in Britain starting in 597 brought the Roman alphabet, which was widely adopted. As Christianity spread, with Latin used in church services, hundreds of Latin words crept into the English language. These include bishop, abbot, candle, and angel. The Viking invaders of the 10th and 11th centuries added various Scandinavian or Old Norse words to the language.

The Norman invasion in 1066 had a huge impact on the English language, bringing thousands of French terms into everyday use. For nearly 150 years, the new nobility and most of the church hierarchy were French-speaking Normans until Britain lost control of Normandy (France) in 1204. These additions account for the rich vocabulary of the English language today.

MIDDLE ENGLISH

The language used between approximately 1150 and 1500 is today known as Middle English. During the late 14th century, English rather than French

Shelta is the dialect used by the ethnic gypsies in Britain and Ireland. It is derived from Irish Gaelic and Old English, possibly via Celtic. Some English slang words are derived from Shelta. An example is the word gammy, meaning lame, which is derived from the Shelta word gyami.

was taught in schools and used in law courts. King Henry IV (1399–1413) was the first English king whose main language was English. By the early 14th century, the dialect of London had become a recognized standard as exemplified in the works of Geoffrey Chaucer, notably in the *Canterbury Tales*.

An illustration of the knight (center), plowman (right), and clerk (left) from *The Canterbury Tales*, which was written in the 14th century.

PLACE NAMES

Many place names recall the groups that colonized Britain over the centuries.

Celtic names are common for most English rivers; *avon* is the Celtic word for river. Esk, Exe, Thames, and Wye are also Celtic words. London is a Celtic place name, after a person called Londinos. *Barr* means hill, *torr* means high rock or peak, *pill* means tide or creek, and the word *Llan* or *Lan* means church in Wales or Cornwall.

Some Roman settlements are easily identifiable. Town names ending in -caster or -chester, such as Doncaster or Manchester, come from the Latin word *castra*, meaning army camp.

Several Anglo-Saxon settlements can be identified by common suffixes in place names: -ham, as in Chippenham, means farm, homestead, estate, village, or manor; -leah, or -ley means woodland and subsequently, a clearing in the woods. The suffix -ing, as in Worthing, means people of. Finally, the suffix -ingham, as in Nottingham, means settlement of a people, and -ington, as in Warrington, means farm or settlement associated with a people.

Scandinavian place names, which are found predominantly in the eastern side of Britain, can sometimes be identified by suffixes: -by means farm, as in Whitby; -thorp means outlying farm or secondary settlement; and -thwaite, for example Applethwaite, means an isolated piece of land.

A few French or Norman place names can be identified and are often pronounced in a manner totally different from English usage: Richmond, Beaumont, and Beaulieu.

THE WELSH LANGUAGE

Just over 20 percent of the population of Wales can speak Welsh, but many more understand it. Road signs and town names are all in Welsh, often with very different renderings from the English names.

Welsh is a phonetic language, one of the Celtic languages similar to French Breton and to the Cornish language, which died out completely in the 18th century. The letters "j", "k", "q", "v", "x", and "z" do not appear in Welsh. "W" and "i" can be both vowel and consonant; when used as a vowel, "w" is pronounced "oo" as in "put," but when it is used as a consonant, "w" is pronounced as in the word "well." "Y" is used as a vowel, pronounced "uh." "Ch" is pronounced as in the Scottish "loch," "f" is pronounced "v," "ff" renders the English "f" sound, "dd" is pronounced as "th," and "ll" roughly as "thl."

The word "Welsh" means stranger. A few other terms are: *dydd da* (thuhd-dar), meaning good day; *sut mae* (soot-may), meaning how are you; and *croeso* (kro-wee-so), which is used to extend a welcome.

GAELIC

Only about 58,650 people in Scotland speak Gaelic, and they are found predominantly in the Highlands. Like Welsh, Gaelic is also a Celtic language and was brought from Ireland to Scotland during the fifth century. Unlike Welsh, the language has no official status in Scotland and is not taught in schools. Gaelic words now used widely in English include bard, glen, bog, slogan, whisky, brogue, clan, and loch.

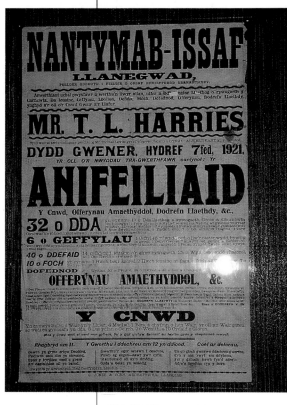

The Welsh newspaper, *Nantymab-Isaaf,* at the museum in Cardiff.

ENGLISH DIALECTS AND ACCENTS

The way a person speaks is a good indication of where he or she comes from. A Welsh person speaks English with a musical, singsong lilt, while a Scottish person has a pronounced, almost guttural accent. Those who come from the West Country widen vowels and pronounce "s" as "z," so that "cider" becomes "zoyder." Midlands accents in the Birmingham area are flatter and more nasal.

Many of these local variations are the result of centuries of regional developments in the English language. For example, in a wide area north of the Humber River, across Yorkshire and over the border to Scotland, people still say "lang" rather than "long." In an area stretching farther south into Derbyshire and Nottinghamshire, words such as "night," "right," and "fright" are pronounced with an "ee" sound as in "neat." The southern pronunciation of a long "ah" in "past," "path," and "laugh" never progressed beyond a diagonal line from the Wash in East Anglia to Wales; north of that line people tend to use a short "a" as in "flat" for these words.

COCKNEY RHYMING SLANG

A witty and sharp form of slang has evolved in the East End of London, of which many common expressions are now widely known in Britain and abroad. The slang depends on the rhyme on the last word of a pair; to add confusion, often only the first word of the pair is actually spoken. In this list, the words in parentheses are not said aloud.

Rhyming Slang	Meaning
Trouble [and strife]	wife
Butcher's [hook]	look
Whistle [and flute]	suit
Ball of chalk	walk
Dog [and bone]	telephone
Bowl of water	daughter
Apples [and pears]	stairs
Dicky [dirt]	shirt
Half inch	pinch (steal)
Rosy Lea	tea
Cain and Abel	table
Jam jar	car
Sausage [and mash]	cash
Pen [and ink]	stink
Tit [for tat]	hat

Together with the age-old local dialects, Britain's immigrant population has brought further diversity and richness to English usage. For example, reggae and rap music generally feature in the rich English patois of the West Indian population.

Standard English, sometimes called King's or Queen's English, or Received Pronunciation, is the pronunciation generally practiced by those living near London and by most announcers on BBC radio and television. Those from the middle and upper classes generally speak in this manner, with an accent that does not reflect where their family comes from.

The richness and variety of pronunciation and accents is a major component of the renowned British sense of humor.

ARTS

BRITAIN'S VARIED ARTISTIC heritage is world-renowned, from the plays of William Shakespeare and the paintings of John Constable to the music of The Beatles.

Funding of the arts is controversial. Public spending on subsidies for galleries, theaters, and universities has been reduced. Instead, businesses have been encouraged to sponsor theatrical and musical productions and artistic exhibitions, and money raised by the National Lottery is often used.

CLASSICAL MUSIC

EARLY MUSIC Early English music was mainly written for the Catholic Church. Thomas Tallis under Henry VIII composed music for the new Anglican Church, while his pupil William Byrd wrote numerous madrigals, choral works, and string and keyboard works. In the 17th century, Henry Purcell wrote church music and harpsichord pieces, as well as the operas *Dido and Aeneas* and *The Indian Queen*, all of which combined the older medieval tones and scales of the English tradition with Italian and French styles.

George Friedrich Handel, under the patronage of King George I, composed *Music for the Royal Fireworks, Water Music*, and *The Messiah*.

Opposite: **A painting by English artist William Blake called** *Jacob's Ladder*.

Below: **The Royal Albert Hall in London is a popular place for both classical and modern musical performances, as well as sporting events such as boxing competitions.**

EISTEDDFODS

During the first full week of August the Royal National Eisteddfod (aye-STED-fod) of Wales is held. Its location alternates between North and South Wales and varies each year. The word *eisteddfod* means a meeting of bards, and the festival is a contest for poets, singers, and musicians. All proceedings are in Welsh, although instant translation facilities are available. The Gorsedd or council of bards presides over the occasion, with the Archdruid of Gorsedd officiating. At the end of the week, two ceremonies are held: the chairing ceremony for strict meter verse, for which the winner is awarded the prestigious Bardic Chair; and the crowning ceremony for free verse, for which the winner gains the Bardic Crown.

18TH CENTURY In the early 18th century, Thomas Arne composed *Rule Britannia*, an anthem that is still sung on special occasions. During that century, many philharmonic clubs, concert clubs, and choral societies were formed.

19TH CENTURY AND BEYOND Late 19th-century composers include Arthur Sullivan, who teamed up with W.S. Gilbert to compose 14 operettas. Edward Elgar is famed for his *Enigma Variations*, his haunting *Cello Concerto*, and the *Pomp and Circumstance* marches, which echoed the self-assurance of colonial Britain. Ralph Vaughan Williams was inspired by the rediscovery of English folk songs and featured them in such works as *Fantasia on Greensleeves*.

A new group of contemporary British classical artists have emerged, appealing to a youthful audience as they are young, attractive, and have crossover appeal in their music. They include opera singer Russell Watson, teen prodigy Charlotte Church, and controversial string quartet Bond.

POPULAR MUSIC

Two bands led British popular music onto the world stage in the 1960s—The Beatles and The Rolling Stones. The Beatles, a quartet from Liverpool, had their first hit in 1962 with *Love Me Do* and dominated the British pop music scene until they split up in 1970. They made their grand entrance into the U.S. market with a historic appearance on *The Ed Sullivan Show* in 1964 that was seen by more than 70 million viewers. They are widely regarded as the greatest pop group in history and remain as an iconic musical influence on many of today's bands. The Rolling Stones released *Satisfaction* in 1965, one of many hit singles and albums spanning the next four decades. The legendary rockers have been inducted in the Rock and Roll Hall of Fame.

The 1970s saw the emergence of colorful individual artists such as Elton John and David Bowie and a division between teenagers and older rock fans. Meanwhile, the punk rock movement tried to reclaim rock music for the young and rebellious. Groups such as The Sex Pistols and The Clash shocked people with their rude behavior and outrageous appearance.

In the 1980s came synthesizer rock and bands such as The Eurythmics. One of the biggest pop groups in the 1990s were the Spice Girls, who were equally known for their raunchy music videos, while groups such as Busted, one of the many boy bands appealing to pre-teens that have appeared, topped the charts at the start of the 21st century.

The Beatles—George Harrison, Ringo Starr, John Lennon, and Paul McCartney. Their music, hairstyles, and taste in clothing were highly influential throughout the world at the height of their popularity.

LITERATURE

The breadth and richness of British poetry, prose, and drama stretch over 10 centuries.

POETRY John Milton's 17th-century epic poem *Paradise Lost,* based on biblical references, conjures vivid images of Adam and Eve, hell, and Satan's fall from heaven, while John Donne, who also lived in the 17th century, was a metaphysical poet who used wit and clever puns to convey complex ideas. The 18th-century Scottish poet Robert Burns used his local dialect to describe Scottish scenery and customs in poems such as *Tam O'Shanter* and in songs such as *Auld Lang Syne.* Of the late 18th-century and early 19th-century poets, William Wordsworth's lyrical poetry about the Lake District and John Keats's romantic descriptive verse on the beauties of nature are well known. Early 20th-century war poets Rupert Brooke, Siegfried Sassoon, and Wilfred Owen all describe the horror of the trench warfare of World War I. The Welsh poet Dylan Thomas captivated the lilting musical quality of English spoken by Welsh people; the radio play *Under Milk Wood* is one of his more famous works. Britain has an official poet laureate, appointed by the Queen to write official poetry on state occasions. The current holder of this office is Andrew Motion.

PROSE Prose writers include Samuel Johnson (18th century), who wrote essays on issues of contemporary interest, and Sir Winston Churchill (20th century), who wrote *History of the English-Speaking Peoples*, a four-volume history of Britain from Roman times until Queen Victoria's reign. Novels became popular during the 19th century, with carefully crafted social observations by Jane Austen, romantic tales by Charlotte Brontë, gritty urban realism from Charles Dickens, and tragic rural pathos from Thomas Hardy. Twentieth-century novels include satires by Evelyn Waugh, tales of the sea from Joseph Conrad, working-class sensuality from D.H. Lawrence, and Graham Greene's movie-like narrative techniques. Prestigious literary prizes are awarded annually for original works of fiction, generating widespread interest in new writing. Novelists such as Salman Rushdie, Martin Amis, Julian Barnes, and A.S. Byatt are notable writers of today.

PLAYS British plays include the comedies of Ben Jonson in the 16th century, which were commentaries on flaws in the human character, and the witty social satires of Richard Sheridan and Oliver Goldsmith in the 18th century. Modern playwrights include Harold Pinter, whose writing includes themes of menace, hatred, and isolation. Alan Ayckbourn is known for his detailed portrayals of lower middle-class characters, and Alan Bennett, another keen observer of manners and mores, writes plays, television monologues, and radio pieces.

Portrait of the Polish-born English novelist Joseph Conrad, whose novels include *Lord Jim* and *Nostromo*.

WILLIAM SHAKESPEARE

William Shakespeare holds a central place in British theater. Between 1588 and 1613, he wrote 37 plays, over 150 sonnets, and numerous poems. The Royal Shakespeare Company, founded in 1879, has two theaters devoted to his works: the Swan Theatre in Stratford-on-Avon, his town of birth; and the Globe Theatre in London. While the language used is different from modern English, the themes and characters are vibrant and relevant four centuries later.

The historical plays, narratives of the lives of certain English kings, are thought to have been written in the late 16th century during the reign of Queen Elizabeth I. They all help to explain her reign by glorifying her ancestors, such as Henry V and the Duke of Richmond (later Henry VII), and vilifying those monarchs they ousted, such as Richard III. Shakespeare also wrote several other historical dramas based on classical tales such as *Julius Caesar* and *Antony and Cleopatra*, using well-known plots but increasing their drama by adding tragic pathos to the central characters.

The comedies are generally light-hearted tales of love, with many a twist and turn before a happy ending. These plays often feature strong-minded women and somewhat ineffectual men, and rely less on plausible characterization or plot when compared to the histories and tragedies. They often contain observations on the lower ranks of society, often with humorous characters speaking in prose rather than verse.

Shakespeare's tragedies, in particular *Macbeth*, *Othello*, *Hamlet*, and *King Lear*, are his crowning achievement, all written in his later years. In each of them he develops a central tragic hero dominated by a fierce emotion that leads to his eventual downfall: ambition in *Macbeth*, jealousy in *Othello*, revenge in *Hamlet*, and pride in *King Lear*.

THEATER

London's West End is theater land, with over 100 theaters near Shaftesbury Avenue and Covent Garden. Mainstream musicals are popular, particularly those by Andrew Lloyd Webber. The National Theatre on London's South Bank offers a wide range of contemporary and classical plays at its three repertory theaters. Many towns have theaters that either stage productions by their own companies or host touring groups. Fringe theater (not mainstream) is well-represented on student campuses and in locations such as Stratford Theatre in East London, the Royal Court in Sloane Square, and the Lyric in Hammersmith. Manchester's Royal Exchange Theatre also regularly stages fringe theater, as does Edinburgh's Traverse Theatre.

The Edinburgh Arts Festival every August presents all types of theatrical performances, both mainstream and fringe, to give opportunities to young playwrights to have their works performed. Chichester also has an annual summer theater festival. During summer, open-air performances of plays by Shakespeare are held in London's Regent's Park.

The West End is the heart of London's entertainment district. Shaftesbury Avenue is the center of theater land—the Lyric Theatre was designed in 1888, while the Globe and Apollo theaters opened in the early 20th century.

FILM AND TELEVISION

The Ealing comedies of the 1950s, including *Passport to Pimlico* and *The Titfield Thunderbolt*, were some of Britain's early cinematic triumphs. In the 1980s, Richard Attenborough's *Gandhi*, David Putnam's *Chariots of Fire*, and Merchant Ivory's *Heat and Dust* and *A Room with a View* were highly successful and award-winning epics.

The romantic comedies of Richard Curtis and Working Title films—*Four Weddings and a Funeral*, *Notting Hill*, *Bridget Jones's Diary*, and *Love Actually*—using British actors, filmed in Britain and celebrating British culture, achieved major worldwide box-office success. The *Harry Potter* films, based on J.K. Rowling's phenomenally successful children's book series, have again brought success to the British film industry.

The BBC is known for well-produced television serials and soap operas. Such works include *Brideshead Revisited*, *The Jewel in the Crown*, *Singing Detective*, and *Eastenders*. The independent television channels also produce serials, soap operas, and films. Channel Four, in particular, funds and screens films by new screenwriters and directors.

Britain has a strong tradition of television comedy, such as the classic *Monty Python* series, but just as in the United States, reality television programs, with real people in real-life settings, have become extremely popular and are overtaking traditional programming.

PAINTING

Portraiture was the only branch of painting to survive in England after the Reformation, when religious works of art were prohibited. Under Henry VIII, Hans Holbein the Younger became court painter and depicted many members of the royal household. Nicholas Hilliard painted miniature portraits during Elizabeth I's reign, and Anthony Van Dyck painted

Britain has two monuments dedicated to the history and development of cinema and photography. In London, the National Film Theater is at the South Bank Center, and the National Museum of Photography, Film, and Television is found in Bradford, Yorkshire.

memorable portraits of the early Stuart monarchs.

During the 18th century, William Hogarth painted sequences of moralistic scenes, decrying the sins of alcohol and other vices. Joshua Reynolds and Thomas Gainsborough both painted portraits of wealthy patrons, the former also depicting mythological and historical scenes, the latter trying landscapes.

Britain's best-known exponents of landscape painting are John Constable and J.M.W. Turner. Constable's *The Hay-Wain*, painted in 1821, is an example of his search for truth and realism. In contrast, Turner painted nature as if it expressed human emotions, using light to highly dramatic effect in paintings such as *Peace: Burial at Sea*.

Many of these paintings are on display at the Clore Gallery in London's Tate Britain museum. A new gallery called Tate Modern opened in a disused power station in 2000. It is London's most avant-garde gallery and often has highly controversial exhibitions. Every year the Royal Academy of Arts showcases upcoming talent in an annual summer exhibition.

ARCHITECTURE

Britain's rich architectural heritage is highly varied, stretching back over 10 centuries of religious, civic, business, and domestic styles. The Tower of London and Durham Cathedral are examples of 11th-century Norman style. Exeter Cathedral shows the later Decorated style of English Gothic architecture (1350–1400), while King's College Chapel in Cambridge, built in 1446, is done in the Perpendicular style.

Inigo Jones in the early 17th century developed the Continental Palladian style in buildings such as the Queen's House in Greenwich. Sir Christopher Wren, also a 17th-century architect, left a legacy of 52 city churches, including Saint Paul's Cathedral, which was built after the Fire of London in 1666, and another four churches outside the City of London. He was influenced by the Catholic Baroque architecture of the time but evolved a more restrained form in his work. Sir John Vanbrugh's grandiose Blenheim Palace was similarly Baroque in style, as were Nicholas Hawksmoor's London churches, including Christ Church at the Spitalfields.

The curving Georgian-style Royal Crescent in Bath was designed by John Wood the Younger around 1775. The whole city is an architectural delight. Edinburgh's New Town is another example of the same architectural style. Robert Adam's Classical style is typified by Syon House in Middlesex. Striking examples of Victorian architecture remain in Sir George Gilbert Scott's Saint Pancras Railway Station and Albert Memorial. The Houses of Parliament, by Charles Barry, is also a fine example of Victorian design.

Sir Edwin Lutyens, designer of the colonial city of New Delhi in India, created dream-like country houses using arts-and-crafts techniques in the early 20th century. Modern British architects include Norman Foster, James Stirling, and Richard Rogers. Modern buildings in London by Foster and Partners include the Swiss Re building, commonly known as the gherkin, and the City Hall building on the South Bank. The London Eye, a ferris wheel providing views of Greater London; the Millennium Bridge, a suspended footbridge over the River Thames; and the Millennium Dome in Greenwich, a huge indoor arena, were built to usher in the 21st century.

The Royal Crescent in Bath is an example of classical Georgian architecture. Bath is one of the most elegant and architecturally distinguished of British cities. Many of its older buildings were bulit of limestone found in the nearby Mendip Hills.

LEISURE

SIR WINSTON CHURCHILL'S comment in 1938 that sports was "the first of all the British amusements" rings true even today. Sports is an integral part of the British way of life: millions of mainly male viewers watch soccer, rugby, cricket, and horse racing on television every weekend. Thousands more attend the weekly or bi-weekly soccer matches during the championship season from late August to May. Others attend the summer international cricket Test matches or the Wimbledon All-England Tennis Championships.

Above: Tourists and locals making the best of the summer sun on Brighton beach.

Opposite: The audience at a play at London's Globe Theatre.

Participation in sports is also popular. At school, children are encouraged to take part in games of soccer or rugby (for boys), hockey, netball and lacrosse (for girls), and cricket (for boys), athletics, running, swimming or tennis in summer. Schools compete in numerous local leagues, as do towns, counties, clubs, pubs, and companies.

Sports funding remains controversial, with sponsorship a major part of most professional and even amateur sports. The costs of running minor league soccer teams are often disproportionately high, with increased safety standards, building requirements, and policing needs.

English soccer (its proper name is Association Football) is played throughout Britain, South America, Europe, Africa, and parts of Asia. The term "soccer" is a corruption of the second syllable of "association."

SOCCER

Soccer, called football in Britain, is the most widely followed sport, with national and international matches televised several times a week and league tables published in the daily newspapers. It is played in schools, colleges, local boroughs, and the national leagues.

English soccer is organized into two principal annual competitions: the League Championship and the Football Association (FA) Cup. The former is divided into four divisions: the Premier League and Divisions One, Two, and Three. Teams score three points for a won game and one point for a draw. The team with the most points at the end of the season wins the championship. At the end of each season, the bottom three teams in each division move down a division, while the top two teams in each division move up. A play-off competition between the next top four teams decides the third team to move up a division. The last team in Division Three is relegated to a minor league.

The FA Cup is a knockout competition where teams must win matches to stay in the competition. There are separate Welsh and Scottish football leagues. England, Scotland, and Wales also take part in the European Championship once every four years. Individual teams can take part in various European competitions if they qualify, while the national teams take part in the World Cup held every four years.

Soccer in England, as in other soccer-playing countries, is occasionally accompanied by incidents of "hooliganism," where supporters get out of control and sometimes get violent, often as a result of a bad decision made by the referee or an unexpected defeat. However, the majority of fans do not behave in this way.

WINTER SPORTS

The game of rugby was started at Rugby School in 1823. Rugby Union, traditionally an amateur game but now moving toward professionalism, has an annual series competition known as the Five Nations Championship played between England, Wales, Scotland, Ireland, and France. Matches for this series, and for international test matches against rugby-playing countries such as Australia, New Zealand, and South Africa, are played on famous grounds: England's Twickenham, Scotland's Murrayfield, and Wales's Millennium Stadium.

Rugby League is a professional game and the players are paid. Each team has 13 players instead of the 15 in Rugby Union, and the rules differ slightly for tackling and in some other respects.

Hockey is played at many schools by both sexes. Lacrosse is played mainly by girls, while cross-country running is also quite popular.

A **Rugby Union** match in progress. According to legend, rugby originated in England in 1823, when a soccer player at the Rugby School in Rugby, Warwickshire, ran holding the ball instead of kicking it.

Cricket has a large following in Britain and in former British colonies, such as the West Indies, India, Sri Lanka, Australia, and New Zealand.

SUMMER SPORTS

During summer, tennis and cricket matches are played, and running, swimming, and water sports are popular. Tennis clubs abound, particularly in the southern counties. The All England Championships have been held at Wimbledon since 1877.

Cricket is a game played by two teams of 11 players on a large field, using a red leather ball and a flat wooden bat. The teams bat and bowl alternately. Runs are scored by two batsmen running between the two wickets—three vertical sticks in the ground known as stumps, and two smaller sticks (bails) resting between them. The batsmen can be out of the game in a number of ways such as by fielding positions that limit the number of runs made and by bowling strategies that bowl the wickets down. The team scoring the most runs wins the game. Test matches (international games) can last for five days and still often end with a draw.

Horse racing and betting on races are fairly popular in Britain. Racing takes place from the end of March to the first week of November.

Races at Royal Ascot are noted for the hats worn by spectators as much as for the horse racing itself. The Queen and other members of the royal family often have their own horses running in the Royal Ascot races.

National Hunt races, over hurdles or larger fences, take place between February and June. The most important races are the Cheltenham Gold Cup, and the Grand National at Aintree near Liverpool, which is the best-known steeplechase. Local hunts raise money and run their own point-to-point steeplechases during this period.

Competitions testing the riders' skill at cross-country, horsemanship, and jumping take place at Burghley and Badminton annually. Horse shows are held across Britain during the summer months, ranging from small village contests to the Royal Windsor Horse Show and the Royal International Horse Show at Hickstead in West Sussex.

Greyhound race tracks are located in big cities. Large sums of money are bet on favored animals as they pursue a "hare" around a circular track.

Formula One auto racing takes place at Silverstone north of London and at Donington Park in the Midlands.

British race-car driver Nigel Mansell In a Williams-Renault car at the Silverstone race track.

Above: **Rock climbing is a popular pastime in rocky areas of the countryside.**

Opposite: **Accompanied by foxhounds, riders and huntsmen set out for a day's hunting.**

OUTDOOR PURSUITS

Walking is an extremely popular sport. Even in the pouring rain, groups of walkers clad in waterproof anoraks and boots, often accompanied by dogs, can be seen walking across fields and moors and along river banks. There are several long-distance footpaths, such as the Pennine Way that stretches for 268 miles (431 km) from the Peak District to the Scottish border. Footpaths, bridlepaths for horseback riding, and tracks give walkers the right of way over much of the countryside.

Rock climbing is popular in hilly areas such as around Mount Snowdon in Wales, Froggatt Edge in the Peak District, and numerous locations in the Lake District.

For winter sports enthusiasts, skiing in Scotland is centered around Aviemore, although the snow is unreliable when compared to that in the Alps. On a lesser scale, many families have toboggans to use on slopes in public parks and nearby fields in the winter. Many people skate on frozen ponds and rivers.

Sailing is popular, especially on the southern coast and on the Isle of Wight, where the Cowes Week Regatta takes place in early August. Tall ship races leave from Plymouth, Falmouth, and Southampton in July and August. Dinghy sailing, windsurfing, and water skiing take place on some reservoirs and lakes during summer.

FIELD SPORTS

Hunting, shooting, and fishing are called field sports. Each sport has its season, arranged in order to allow the quarry time to breed. Fishing is by

far the national pastime, with more participants than even watch soccer matches. Fishing spots range from canals and reservoirs to rivers where Scottish salmon can be caught.

There are several different types of hunting. Hunters meet and pursue foxes once or twice a week, between November and March, accompanied by huntsmen and followers on horseback. Between August and October, cub hunting, a less formal type of fox hunting, takes place. Hares are hunted using beagles or hounds. Deer are hunted with hounds in the West Country, where the sport is known as stag hunting, and with rifles in the Scottish highlands, where it is called deer stalking.

In all forms of hunting, the animals pursued are generally viewed as pests by the local farmers and landowners, who argue that hunting helps reduce their numbers. Those who oppose hunting sometimes sabotage hunts by confusing the scent and disrupting the hunts. Fox hunting is banned in Scotland; the UK Parliament has voted to outlaw it.

Oscar Wilde described fox hunting as "the unspeakable in full pursuit of the uneatable."

GARDENS

Gardening is a major hobby for many people. Many homes have a small plot of land, whether a suburban garden, an allotment at some distance from one's house or apartment, or a larger country garden. Newspapers have a regular column on gardening tips, and numerous gardening books line shelves of libraries and bookshops. A degree of competitiveness can take hold as neighbors try to outdo one another, especially during preparations for local horticultural shows.

Over 3,000 individual gardens are open to the public under a National Gardens Scheme. They include ordinary suburban gardens and those of large country houses. Examples of Elizabethan knot gardens (*left*), medieval walled enclosures of fruit trees, roses and herbs, well-tended mazes, 18th-century landscaped gardens, and cottage gardens with mixed vegetables and flowers abound throughout the country. Agricultural and horticultural shows are held throughout the summer months, and classes in gardening and flower arranging, which offer a wealth of ideas to the avid gardener, are available in the evenings.

VACATIONS

Working people are entitled to at least 20 days of paid leave a year by EU employment law, which they refer to as holidays. Workers in large manufacturing industries often must take their vacation when the plant is shut for maintenance, and many industrial towns have vacation, or "wakes," weeks during the school vacations so that family members in different jobs can take vacations at the same time. Among workers in the service sector, vacation times are more flexible.

There are numerous vacation spots within Britain. The Lake District, Yorkshire Dales, and Peak District are popular areas for walking and climbing trips. Devon and Cornwall's rugged coasts and inland moorlands draw tourists from elsewhere in Britain as well as from abroad. The resorts

A vacation on the beach at picturesque Saint Ives in Cornwall.

of the southern coast are popular destinations for those from the Greater London area. Workers from the industrial towns of Lancashire used to go on vacation in Blackpool on the western coast, while those from the industrial towns of Yorkshire, on the other side of the Pennines, used to go to Skegness on the eastern coast.

Many families take advantage of very competitively priced package tours and budget airline flights to foreign destinations. Spain remains a favorite spot for British tourists, and many hotels on the Costa Brava offer British tourists fish and chips, strong Indian tea, and British beer. The Canary Islands, Greece, Italy, and other European destinations are also popular, and an increasing number of Britons travel to the Alps or to the United States for winter skiing vacations.

Washing the car on a Sunday morning.

OTHER LEISURE ACTIVITIES

The British spend much of their leisure time engaged in home-based activities: listening to music, watching television, playing video games, and gardening. Making home improvements is a popular leisure activity as well as a money-saving practice. Many men spend their weekends tinkering with motorbikes and cars, repairing or working on their vehicles in the garage and backyard.

The British love of animals is legendary, and many British families keep pets, such as dogs, cats, goldfish, and parakeets.

During children's school vacations, visits to local attractions, theme parks, and youth clubs are popular, although these vary by family and area. Some schools, youth groups, churches, and commercial organizations arrange holiday camps and vacation activities for children. Organizations such as the Brownies or Girl Guides also have vacation activities for their members.

There are over 70,000 public houses or pubs in England and Wales, and

114

People socialize and play games in pubs.

several thousand more in Scotland. Pubs are major focal points of social life, formerly mainly for men, but increasingly for women, too. Pubs are open from Monday to Saturday from 11:00 A.M. to 11:00 P.M. On Sundays, they open from noon to 10:30 P.M. or 11:00 P.M. Children accompanied by adults who wish to have a meal are admitted to pubs at the individual landlord's discretion. Many pubs serve high-quality food and a variety of snacks at reasonable prices.

Some pubs provide games for their customers' entertainment: perhaps a dart board, a pool or billiards table, sets of dominoes, and other board games may be found, along with pinball and slot machines.

Libraries remain free, run by local councils, and have a fairly wide selections of books, and in some libraries, records, compact discs, video tapes, and cassettes. Most libraries have Internet access. Continuing education classes for adults, mainly in urban centers, are also available in a number of subjects. Going to the theater, ten-pin bowling, or out for a meal are common leisure activities.

FESTIVALS

SEVERAL DATES ARE CELEBRATED throughout Britain. The beginning of a new year is celebrated everywhere, especially in Scotland, where January 1 is called Hogmanay. An old tradition that might be observed by some families is eating haggis (spiced minced meat boiled in a sheep's stomach) before the "first footing." This custom, now rarely practiced, involves a tall man who visits homes bearing gifts and best wishes and tries to be the first foot in the door in the new year. Another Scottish celebration, Burns Night, named after the poet Robert Burns, occurs on January 25. On this day banquets are held with speeches, drinking, singing, recitations, and dancing.

Halloween, which falls on October 31, is popular with children, who dress up in costumes and ask neighbors to choose between "trick" or "treat." November 5 is Guy Fawkes Day. Throughout England, bonfires are lit, old clothes are turned into effigies, and fireworks are set off to commemorate the failure of a plot in 1605 to blow up Parliament. November 11 is Armistice Day, held to remember those who died in the two world wars. A procession of approximately 1,000 ex-servicemen is held, led by the Queen and attended by political leaders. Wreaths are laid on the Cenotaph war memorial in Whitehall, and a two-minute silence to honor the war dead is observed. In addition, red paper poppies are worn on jackets in support of war veterans.

Above: **Fireworks over the city of Edinburgh on New Year's Eve.**

Opposite: **Morris dancers in England perform on May Day.**

117

Two Chelsea Pensioners in full uniform and medals having a drink after the annual parade at the Royal Hospital Chelsea.

LONDON FESTIVALS

Several parades and occasions are peculiar to London and show some of Britain's pomp and ceremony.

Around May 29 there is a parade at the Royal Hospital Chelsea, a veteran soldiers' hospital founded in 1692 by King Charles II. Called the Chelsea Pensioners, the veterans, often in their 80s, stand stiffly proud, showing numerous battlefield medals as they are greeted by a member of the royal family. In late May, the Chelsea Flower Show takes place on the grounds of the Royal Hospital. The show is attended by thousands of amateur gardeners.

The Notting Hill Carnival, a vibrant street festival of floats, stalls, and music that celebrate West Indian culture, has been held in northern London on the last weekend of August since 1964. It is a predominantly Afro-Caribbean affair, with steel bands and sideshows and features

Caribbean food specialties. There is sometimes friction between the local residents and participants as the former have trouble parking their cars and petty theft incidents occur.

The London Marathon starts in Blackheath and ends on The Mall, in April, and attracts 30,000 runners and thousands of spectators annually. The London-to-Brighton vintage car rally takes place every November, in celebration of the raising of the speed limit from 4 to 12 miles per hour (6 to 19 km per hour) in 1896. To enter the rally, cars must have been built before January 1, 1905.

One of the most spectacular London festivals is the Lord Mayor's Show, held on the second Saturday of November. The Lord Mayor of London, an elected official from the business community, riding in a gold state coach built in 1757 that is drawn by three pairs of Shire horses, travels from the Guildhall to the Royal Courts of Justice in the Strand. The 12 great city livery companies, each with royal charters dating back several centuries, follow his coach in decorated floats. The Lord Mayor's banquet is then held in the Guildhall on the Monday after the show. At other times of the year, he hosts dinners in the Mansion House. Despite the centuries-old ceremony and dress, the current views of the City of London's powerful financial community are aired at these banquets, and political leaders use the event as a platform for their own policies.

Ceremonial guards waiting for the Lord Mayor of London to participate in the Lord Mayor's Show in November.

Above: **The nativity scene at Christmas.**

Opposite: **Morris dancers play accordions.**

CHRISTIAN FESTIVALS

During Advent, carol services are held in churches, nativity plays and pantomimes are performed in schools and theaters, street decorations appear in town centers, and many families buy Christmas trees to decorate.

Every family's Christmas routine is different, but most involve children leaving stockings by chimneys or at the ends of their beds; they believe that Santa Claus will fill the stockings with gifts the night before Christmas. Presents are exchanged with family and friends. A traditional meal of roast turkey, followed by Christmas pudding, is eaten at lunch or suppertime.

Ash Wednesday, the first day of Lent, is so called because priests anoint their congregations with ashes as a sign of penitence. Lent itself, the 40-day period before Easter Sunday, is a time when more devout Christians may make personal sacrifices to emulate Jesus.

On Maundy Thursday, the day before Good Friday, the Queen distributes specially minted coins—the same amount as her age—to poor men and women of her age at a different church every year. On Good Friday, churches hold services all day and devout Christians pray for the three hours when Jesus was believed to be on the cross.

The word Easter comes from the name of a Saxon goddess Eastre, whose festival was held in the spring. The giving of chocolate eggs at this time is more connected to the pagan worship of the goddess Eastre than to any Christian belief. In some areas, egg-rolling contests are held on Easter Monday; in others, eggs are hidden in gardens and houses for children to find.

COUNTRY FESTIVALS

Various regions celebrate rural festivities that date back over many centuries.

PLOUGH MONDAY In some areas, Plough Monday, the Monday after Epiphany on January 6, is celebrated as the traditional resumption of plowing after the 12 days of Christmas celebrations have ended.

SUMMER SHOWS Appleby Horse Fair, a horse sale, is held every June in a picturesque village in the Lake District. A large proportion of villages and counties hold rural fêtes, shows, or contests during the summer months, generally for charity. Harvest festivals are held in churches throughout the country in late August, and churches are decorated with agricultural produce. In the West Country a Saxon custom of wassailing—wishing good health to the apple trees and cider drinkers—continues on January 17.

FOLK DANCE Morris dancing, a type of English folk dance based on the European Morisca, a Moorish dance, came to be associated with May Games (which takes place on May 1), and with the characters from Robin Hood (as seen in the dancers' costumes). The dance is performed by men, usually accompanied by music from an accordion and drums, and is said to have derived from pagan fertility rites.

The Church took over many such pagan rituals.

An elaborately decorated well in the Derbyshire village of Hope.

In Derbyshire villages, for example, the custom of dressing water wells takes place after Ascension Day in July and August. Pictorial panels of flowers are placed next to the wells to give thanks for the water supply.

ROYAL PAGEANTRY

The British love of ceremony is best exemplified by the role of the royal family. Their daily appointments are listed in *The Times* newspaper court circular column. There are various regular and customary occasions when the public can view royal pageantry.

- The Changing of the Guard at Buckingham Palace takes place daily (during spring and summer) and on alternate days (during the fall and winter) at 11:30 A.M. The New Guard replaces the Old during this ceremony popular with tourists.

- The Trooping of the Colour is held on a Saturday in early June to celebrate the queen's official birthday. The color, or standard flag, of each regiment has been symbolic of its fighting unity since the British Army was remodeled under Oliver Cromwell. The queen, seated in a horse-drawn carriage, inspects the troops of her personal guard.

- The State Opening of Parliament occurs every November after the long summer recess; the ceremony has scarcely changed since the 16th century. The queen travels from Buckingham Palace in the Irish State Coach, and reads from the throne the Gracious Speech—a statement of the current government's legislative program for the coming year.

- Cannon salutes are fired from the Tower of London for the queen's official (June) and actual (April) birthdays, the birthday of the Duke of Edinburgh, the State Opening of Parliament, and the Accession and Coronation days. The national anthem has traditionally been played on BBC radio on these days.

- Investitures of knights and other ranks take place throughout the year. Garter Day, an impressive ceremony at Windsor Castle held every June, is the day when any new members, chosen by the queen, are admitted into the Order of the Garter (the highest order of knighthood).

- Irregular occasions are the focus of much ceremony: the Queen's Silver Jubilee Year in 1977 after 25 years and her Golden Jubilee in 2002 after 50 years on the throne; the various royal weddings; and the funerals of Diana, Princess of Wales, in 1997 and Queen Elizabeth, the Queen Mother, in 2002.

FOOD

TRADITIONAL BRITISH FOOD has a reputation for being rather unimaginative and bland. However, many British cooks are becoming more adventurous in food preparation.

It is hard to identify a typical British diet. Italian dishes such as pasta and pizza are very mainstream, and so are a variety of spicy dishes such as Indian and Thai curries. Britain's rich heritage of immigration is reflected in the variety of instant meals and exotic ingredients available in supermarkets.

Cookery, food, and eating out are widespread interests. Britain has a number of television celebrity chefs, and recipe books and cookery magazines sell in large numbers. *The Times* newspaper now has a daily recipe column.

Above: **A family having Sunday lunch.**

Opposite: **The town of Melton Mowbray in Leicestershire is well-known for its pork pies.**

TRADITIONAL BRITISH FOOD

The traditional British breakfast is a hearty affair, requiring a huge appetite and ample time. It is usually prepared as a weekend or holiday treat. Grilled or fried pork sausages, sliced bacon, mushrooms, tomatoes, and baked beans are served together with fried, scrambled, or poached eggs, toast, or fried or "eggy" bread. It may be accompanied by regional specialities such as lambs' kidneys; blood pudding, a type of rich sausage; oatcakes, which are flat, pancake-like items; or fried potatoes and cabbage, known as "bubble and squeak."

On normal days, most families have a more continental-type breakfast, consisting of cereal with milk and sugar (porridge in Scotland), followed by toast and marmalade (oatcakes in Scotland). Yogurt and fruit are also popular with weight watchers and the health-conscious.

Lancashire hot pot consists of lamb, onions, potatoes, and seasonings.

MEAL TIMES Most people eat breakfast between 7:00 and 9:00 A.M., and lunch between noon and 1:30 P.M. The family evening meal time varies enormously between households, depending on work schedules, travel times from work to home, and ages of children. It is not uncommon for children to have their evening meal at an earlier time than their parents.

Some families eat their main meal at midday, while others do so in the evening. The dishes served in either case are similar. A popular traditional Sunday lunch is roast beef, mutton, or lamb, accompanied by roast onions, potatoes, and other vegetables. Other British main dishes include steak and kidney pie; Lancashire hot pot, a type of stew; shepherd's pie, minced beef with a mashed potato covering; and toad-in-the-hole, skinned sausages baked in pancake batter. Many people find it easier to buy ready-to-cook frozen or chilled meals from the supermarket, rather than taking the time to prepare a fresh meal after a day's work. Indian chicken tikka masala and Thai green chicken curry are currently the most popular instant meals of this type.

Sandwiches are a popular lunch and are ideal for a quick office break or a school lunchbox. Supermarkets sell pre-packed sandwiches, and sandwich bars in cities make fresh sandwiches to order.

Many traditional puddings are designed to fill hungry stomachs at minimal cost. Examples are bread-and-butter pudding, an egg custard poured over sliced buttered bread with currants and raisins; jam roly-poly, a rolled suet pudding spread with jam and usually served with custard; and rice pudding, long-grain rice baked in milk and sugar.

Local specialties should be sampled when traveling in Britain. Scottish salmon is delicious, whether smoked or poached, and freshly-caught river trout is also excellent. Scottish beef, from cattle raised on the highland moors, has minimal fat and is very tender and tasty. Venison is also available in Scotland. Despite its description, Scottish haggis—sheep's innards, boiled with onions, suet, and seasonings in the skin of a sheep's stomach and served with mashed rutabaga and potatoes—is a real delicacy. Tender Welsh lamb served with mint sauce and vegetables should not be missed. Oysters from East Anglia are a delicacy that is traditionally served only during months with an "r" in them.

Britain has a large confectionery industry. Sweets and chocolates are sold at corner shops, newsstands, and supermarkets, often placed temptingly at child's height. Salty snacks such as potato chips are also popular. Cookies, cakes, and a wide range of bakery products are also popular. Traditionally served at afternoon tea, such products are widely available but efforts are being made to encourage young children to eat fruit and healthier foods instead.

A magnificent spread of food at the Inn on the Park Hotel in London.

EATING OUT

Eating out at a restaurant in Britain has increasingly become a part of social life. Numerous Italian, Greek, Continental, Chinese, and Indian restaurants can be found in most small towns and generally open late to catch people leaving pubs at around 11:00 P.M. who still want a drink or food. A few chains of steak houses serve traditional English food, as do some hotels. Some of the best quality and value in food can be found in pubs where, particularly in country areas, it is possible to enjoy very reasonable traditional English fare, and as well as more adventurous Continental-style cuisine, served simply and quickly. Gourmet pubs, known as "gastropubs," serve fine food at a fraction of high-class restaurant prices in an informal setting. Takeout restaurants are common in Britain. Chinese takeout restaurants are replacing many of Britain's traditional fish and chip shops, and kebab houses are common in many city suburbs. Hamburger chains are widespread and popular.

DRINKS

The custom of afternoon tea was established during the 1840s by the Duchess of Bedford. Gradually, afternoon tea was accompanied by small snacks such as homemade cakes, scones, cookies, sandwiches, toasted muffins, or crumpets.

The British consume about one-fifth of the world's total tea exports. The preferred brew is Indian or Sri Lankan rather than Chinese.

With 1,200 different brands available, beer is a national drink, made from hops and matured in

A traditional English afternoon tea is a holiday treat rather than an everyday occurrence.

oak casks. Most British beer is bitter. Stout and mild beer are also available. A fairly high quality of bitter can now be found in most pubs, after the efforts of the Campaign for Real Ale reasserted the customer's need to drink traditionally brewed and kept ale. Real, or traditionally brewed, ale is always served at room temperature. Lagers, imported from Germany, Belgium, and Denmark, are increasingly popular. Like American beer, lagers are served cold.

In the West Country, cider is brewed from apples; some delicious rough local brews known as scrumpy are extremely strong. Wine is produced in Kent and Sussex in the south of England, where commercial vineyards have proved moderately successful in penetrating the local market. There are also strong homemade wines made from elderberry or other wild flowers.

Whiskies from Scotland's 100 distilleries remain a profitable export, and numerous blended whiskies, and single and double malt whiskies are matured on Scottish islands such as Jura and Islay. Of other distilled spirits, gin from juniper berries is a profitable export. Carbonated drinks are popular with children and teenagers.

TOAD-IN-THE-HOLE

This filling winter dish, served for either lunch or supper, is a very traditional English choice that is making a comeback in some restaurants and pubs. It is based on pancake mixture, from which Yorkshire Pudding is made (traditionally served with an English roast beef). It is best made with sausages with a lot of flavor, and is often served with gravy and, sometimes, mashed potatoes and peas. Some people eat it as a special treat on Saint George's Day.

When preparing the dish, it is important to keep the oven extremely hot, and not to open the oven door ahead of time, or the batter will not rise properly. The recipe below serves four.

1 pound (450 g) skinless sausages
1 ounce (30 g) cooking fat, lard, or some
    vegetable oil
4 ounces (120 g) plain flour
$^1/_2$ teaspoon salt
1 medium-sized egg
1 cup milk, made up to 2 cups with water

Heat the oven to 400°F (220°C). Put the sausages and fat in a 7 x 11 inch (17 x 27 cm) baking dish and heat in the oven for 5 minutes. Alternatively, chop each sausage into four pieces and put two or three pieces into individual muffin tins. Make sure that there is sufficient lard in each muffin tin.

Sift the flour and salt into a bowl, make a well, and break in the egg. Mix and stir in the liquid gradually, beating with a whisk until it is smooth and bubbly.

Add the batter quickly to the partly cooked sausages and return to the oven.

Bake one individual pie for 30 to 35 minutes, or the individual muffin ones for 20 to 25 minutes until the batter has risen and is brown and firm. Do not open the oven too early—the air will make the batter fall.

BREAD AND BUTTER PUDDING

Another filling and extremely cheap and straightforward dish, this pudding is being rediscovered by restaurants and again becoming increasingly popular. No one, not even the hungriest builder or schoolchild after a football tournament, could still be peckish after eating this dish. Sometimes, rum, marmalade, or minced meat is added to the traditional recipe for a different twist. The recipe below serves four.

Sliced, slightly stale white bread
2 tablespoons soft butter
4 tablespoons raisins or currants
A pinch of nutmeg or cinnamon

2 cups milk
2 eggs
2 tablespoons granulated sugar

Grease a 9-inch (1-liter) pie dish. Cut the crusts off the bread and spread thinly with butter. Cut into squares or triangles and arrange buttered side up in rows in the dish. Sprinkle currants and nutmeg over each level. Arrange the top layer attractively in a pattern. Warm up the milk, but don't let it boil. Beat the eggs and sugar together with a fork and stir in the warmed milk. Pour over the bread and sprinkle a little more sugar on top. Leave to stand for half an hour, then cook in moderate oven at 350°F (180°C) for 30 to 40 minutes until set and browned. Serve hot.

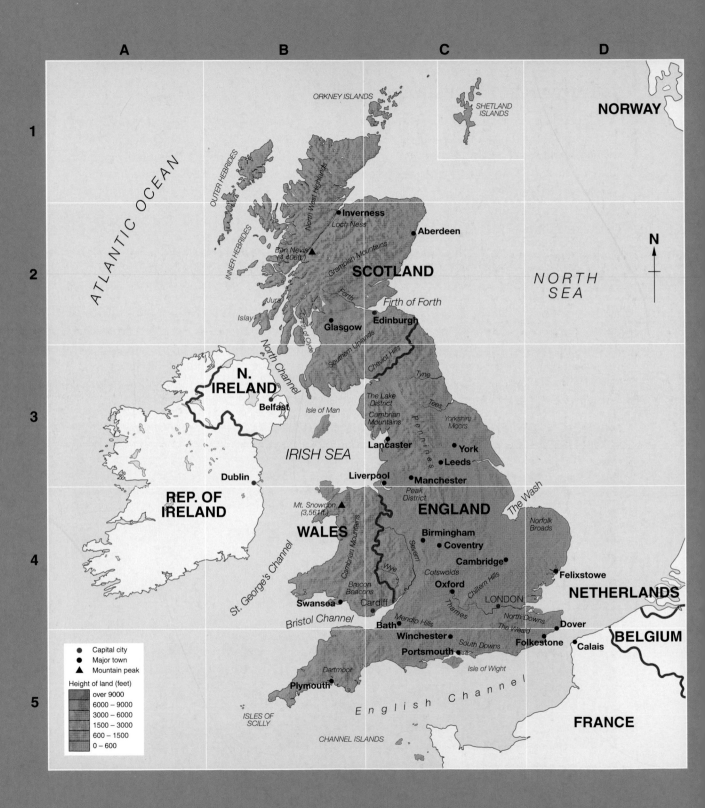

A **B** **C** **D**

1

ORKNEY ISLANDS

SHETLAND ISLANDS

NORWAY

N

ATLANTIC OCEAN

OUTER HEBRIDES

INNER HEBRIDES

North West Highlands

● Inverness
Loch Ness

● **Aberdeen**

Ben Nevis
(4,406ft) ▲

Grampian Mountains

SCOTLAND

NORTH SEA

2

Jura

Islay

Firth of Clyde

Forth

Firth of Forth

● **Glasgow**   ● **Edinburgh**

Southern Uplands

Cheviot Hills

Tyne

North Channel

N. IRELAND

Isle of Man

● **Belfast**

The Lake District

Cumbrian Mountains

Tees

Yorkshire Moors

3

IRISH SEA

● **Lancaster**   ● **York**
● **Leeds**

● Dublin

Pennines

● **Liverpool**   ● **Manchester**

REP. OF IRELAND

Peak District

The Wash

Mt. Snowdon ▲
(3,561ft)

ENGLAND

Norfolk Broads

WALES

Cambrian Mountains

● **Birmingham**
● **Coventry**

Severn

● **Cambridge**

Cotswolds

Wye

Chiltern Hills

● Felixstowe

Brecon Beacons

● **Oxford**

NETHERLANDS

4

St. George's Channel

● **Swansea**   ● Cardiff

LONDON

Thames

North Downs

The Weald

● **Dover**

Bristol Channel

● **Bath**

Mendip Hills

South Downs

● Folkestone

BELGIUM

● **Winchester**

● Calais

Dartmoor

● **Portsmouth**

Isle of Wight

● **Plymouth**

E n g l i s h   C h a n n e l

5

ISLES OF SCILLY

CHANNEL ISLANDS

FRANCE

● Capital city
● Major town
▲ Mountain peak

Height of land (feet)
over 9000
6000 – 9000
3000 – 6000
1500 – 3000
600 – 1500
0 – 600

MAP OF BRITAIN

Aberdeen, C2
Atlantic Ocean, A1–A2

Bath, C4
Belfast, B3
Belgium, D4–D5
Ben Nevis, B2
Birmingham, C4
Brecon Beacons, B4–C4
Bristol Channel, B4

Calais, D5
Cambrian Mountains, B4
Cambridge, C4
Cardiff, C4
Channel Islands, C5
Cheviot Hills, C3
Chiltern Hills, C4
Cotswolds, C4
Coventry, C4
Cumbrian Mountains, C3

Dartmoor, B5
Dover, D4
Dublin, B3

Edinburgh, C2
England, C4
English Channel, B5–C5

Felixstowe, D4
Folkestone, D5
Firth of Clyde, B2–B3
Firth of Forth, C2
Forth river, B2
France, C5–D5

Glasgow, B2
Grampian Mountains, B2–C2

Inner Hebrides, B2
Inverness, B2
Irish Sea, B3
Islay, B2
Isle of Man, B3
Isles of Scilly, B5
Isle of Wight, C5

Jura, B2

Lake District, C3
Lancaster, C3
Leeds, C3
Liverpool, C3
Loch Ness, B2
London, C4

Manchester, C3
Mendip Hills, C4
Mount Snowdon, B4

Netherlands, D4

Norfolk Broads, D4
North Channel, B3
North Downs, C4–D4
North Sea
North West Highlands, B1–B2
Northern Ireland, B3
Norway, D1

Orkney Islands, C1
Outer Hebrides, B1
Oxford, C4

Peak District, C4
Pennines, C3
Plymouth, B5
Portsmouth, C5

Republic of Ireland, A3–B3, A4–B4

Saint George's Channel, B4
Scotland, B2–C2
Severn river, C4
Shetland Islands, C1
South Downs, C5
Southern Uplands, B3, C2
Swansea, B4

Tees river, C3
Thames river, C4
Tyne river, C3

Wales, B4
Wash, C4
Weald, C4–C5
Winchester, C5
Wye river, C4

York, C3
Yorkshire Moors, C3

ECONOMIC BRITAIN

Farming
- Barley
- Cattle
- Horticulture
- Sheep
- Wheat

Manufacturing
- Whiskey

Natural Resources
- Oil

Services
- Airport
- Finance
- Information Technology
- Port
- Tourism

ABOUT THE ECONOMY

OVERVIEW
Britain entered the early 21st century with a long period of sustained economic growth, low inflation, and low interest rates and high employment. U.K. GDP is currently rising at 3 percent. While many of Britain's traditional heavy industries, such as coal mining, steel, and iron, have declined over the past 20 years, and manufactured goods and clothing are imported from parts of the world with much lower labor costs, the service, high technology, and tourist sectors have grown enormously.

GROSS DOMESTIC PRODUCT (GDP)
$1.7 trillion (2003)

GDP PER CAPITA
$27,700 (2003)

GDP SECTORS
Agriculture 0.9 percent, industry 26.5 percent, services 72.6 percent (2003)

INFLATION RATE
1.3 percent (August 2004)

CURRENCY
1 pound (GBP) = 100 pence
USD 1 = GBP 0.55 (November 2004)
Notes: 5, 10, 20, 50 pounds
Coins: 1, 2, 5, 10, 20, 50 pence; 1, 2 pounds

AGRICULTURAL PRODUCTS
Wheat, barley, milk, wool, poultry, whiskey, fish, cattle, sheep, potatoes, cereals

INDUSTRIAL PRODUCTS
Cars and car components, aerospace, construction, automation equipment, metals, chemicals, electronics and communications equipment, shipbuilding, textiles

EXPORTS
Manufactured goods, chemical and pharmaceutical goods, fuels, food, beverages, tobacco, services (including banking and stockbroking)

IMPORTS
Manufactured goods, machinery, fuels, foodstuff, clothing

TRADE PARTNERS
United States, Germany, France, Ireland, Netherlands, Belgium, Italy, Spain

MAJOR AIRPORTS
London Heathrow, London Gatwick, Stansted, Manchester, Birmingham, Edinburgh, Aberdeen

MAJOR PORTS
Felixstowe, Folkestone, Dover, London, Portsmouth

WORKFORCE
28.3 million (June 2004)

UNEMPLOYMENT RATE
4.7 percent (November 2004)

CULTURAL BRITAIN

The Lake District
This picturesque area in northwestern England has inspired poets, such as William Wordsworth, and children's authors, such as Beatrix Potter. It is highly popular with tourists, climbers, and walkers.

Royal Armouries Museum
Located in Leeds, the museum has five themed galleries with interactive displays. In summer, there are jousting and falconry demonstrations on the grounds.

Mount Snowdon
Wales' highest mountain and Britain's second highest is served by its own mountain railway.

Ironbridge Gorge Museums
This group of indoor and outdoor museums at Telford in Shropshire celebrates the golden age of the Industrial Revolution.

Glastonbury Festival
An annual event in Glastonbury, this open-air music festival lasts three days in June and features rock band performances, fringe theater shows, and circus and cabaret acts.

Edinburgh Arts Festival
Scotland's capital city, Edinburgh, hosts a world-renowned arts festival in August each year. Mainstream and fringe theater performances, visual arts, and musical performances are the highlights.

Hadrian's Wall
The wall was built by the Romans between A.D. 122 and 128 to keep invading Picts and Scots out of England. Many parts have been made into local farm buildings, but other parts are still recognizable today.

Jorvik Centre
The Viking days are celebrated by the Jorvik Centre in York. Residents walk dressed as Vikings, Viking-age streets are recreated, and archaeological finds are displayed.

Warwick Castle
A major center of power in medieval times, the castle in Warwickshire is very well-preserved, and a visit to its high battlements and furnished rooms gives real insight into former days.

London
Britain's capital city is a center of museums and is home to Westminster Abbey, the Tower of London, numerous theaters, cinemas, concert venues, and galleries.

ABOUT THE CULTURE

OFFICIAL NAME
The United Kingdom of Great Britain and Northern Ireland. Great Britain, or Britain, is the largest of the 2,000 or so islands that make up the British Isles, the group of islands that sits north of France.

NATIONAL FLAG
The Union Flag consists of England's red cross of its patron saint, Saint George, on a white background, combined with Scotland's diagonal white cross of its patron saint, Saint Andrew, on a blue background and Ireland's red diagonal cross of Saint Patrick.

CAPITAL
London

CAPITAL OF WALES
Cardiff (Caerdydd)

CAPITAL OF SCOTLAND
Edinburgh

POPULATION
60.3 million (2004)

LITERACY RATE
99 percent

LIFE EXPECTANCY AT BIRTH
75.8 years for men, 80.8 years for women (2004)

NATIONAL HOLIDAYS
New Year's Day (January 1; and January 2 in Scotland), Good Friday and Easter Monday (March/April), Early May Holiday (Monday nearest to May 1), Spring Bank Holiday (Monday at the end of May, formerly Whitsun), Summer Bank Holiday (last Monday in August), Christmas Day and Boxing Day (December 25 and 26)

ETHNIC GROUPS
English 81.5 percent; Scottish 9.6 percent; Irish 2.4 percent; Welsh 1.9 percent; Ulster 1.8 percent; West Indian, Indian, Pakistani, and other 2.8 percent

RELIGIONS
Christianity, Islam, Hinduism, Sikhism, Judaism

LANGUAGES
English, Welsh, Gaelic

LEADERS IN POLITICS
Winston Churchill, prime minister (1940–45, 1951–55)
Margaret Thatcher, former leader of the Conservative Party, prime minister (1979–90)
Tony Blair, leader of the Labour Party, prime minister (1997–)

LEADERS IN THE ARTS
Norman Foster, architect (1935–)
Andrew Motion, poet laureate (1952–)
Alan Bennett, writer and playwright (1934–)

TIME LINE

IN BRITAIN	IN THE WORLD

6500 B.C.
English Channel formed

4000–1500 B.C.
Henges, including Stonehenge, constructed

753 B.C.
Rome is founded.

116–17 B.C.
The Roman Empire reaches its greatest extent, under Emperor Trajan (98–17).

A.D. 43
Aulus Plautius invades Britain.

122–28
Hadrian's Wall constructed

410
Romans leave Britain

597
Saint Augustine and 40 monks arrive from Rome

A.D. 600
Height of Mayan civilization

871
King Ethelred and his brother, the future King Alfred the Great, defeat the Danes.

1000
The Chinese perfect gunpowder and begin to use it in warfare.

1337
Start of Hundred Years' War

1348
Start of Black Death

1530
Beginning of trans-Atlantic slave trade organized by the Portuguese in Africa.

1536
Act of Union joins Wales to England.

1558–1603
Reign of Elizabeth I of England

1588
The Spanish Armada is defeated.

1620
Pilgrims sail the *Mayflower* to America.

1642
English Civil War

1666
Great Fire of London

1707
Act of Union joins Scotland to England.

1776
U.S. Declaration of Independence

1789–99
The French Revolution

IN BRITAIN	IN THE WORLD
1775–83 American War of Independence	
1793–1815 Britain goes to war against France in the Napoleonic Wars.	
1857 Indian Mutiny, a rebellion against British rule in India	**1861** The U.S. Civil War begins.
	1869 The Suez Canal is opened.
1870 Education Act established, becomes foundation for modern education system	**1914** World War I begins.
1922 BBC, then known as British Broadcasting Company, established	**1939** World War II begins.
	1945 The United States drops atomic bombs on Hiroshima and Nagasaki.
1947 India and Pakistan gain independence.	**1949** The North Atlantic Treaty Organization (NATO) is formed.
1956 Crisis over control of Suez Canal involving Britain, France, and the Middle East	**1957** The Russians launch Sputnik.
	1966–69 The Chinese Cultural Revolution
1982 Falklands War between Argentina and Britain	**1986** Nuclear power disaster at Chernobyl in Ukraine
	1991 Break-up of the Soviet Union
1997 Tony Blair becomes prime minister; death of Diana, Princess of Wales	**1997** Hong Kong is returned to China.
	2001 Terrorists crash planes in New York, Washington, D.C., and Pennsylvania.
	2003 War in Iraq

GLOSSARY

ale
A bitter beer made from rapid fermentation of malt, hops, and yeast at a high temperature.

barrow
A communal burial ground in southern England.

Caledonia
Old name for Scotland.

cockney
Dialect of working-class population of the East End of London.

constitutional monarchy
A political system that legally limits the actions of the king or queen.

devolution
The delegation of certain powers by a central authority to regional governments.

Druids
Ancient order of Celts consisting of learned men who were usually judges, priests, or teachers.

eisteddfod (aye-STED-fod)
Poetry, singing, and musical competition during which all proceedings are held in Welsh.

Gaelic
Celtic language of Scotland and Ireland.

glen
A narrow, secluded valley.

Huguenots
Protestants in France in the 16th and 17th centuries.

loch (LOCK)
Scottish term for deep lakes.

Magna Carta
Historical document that guaranteed political rights and personal liberties in Britain.

operetta
A comical or romantic opera.

peers
Members of the House of Lords, Britain's upper house of parliament.

ria (ree-ah)
A coast characterized by a series of long, narrow, wedge-shaped inlets that widen and deepen uniformly toward the sea.

tartan
A fabric of Scottish origin that has a plaid design and is traditionally made into a kilt.

tor
A high, craggy hill.

weald
A forest or wooded area.

Witan
An Anglo-Saxon council of men that decided on royal succession and other policy matters.

FURTHER INFORMATION

BOOKS

Alibhai-Brown, Yasmin. *Who Do We Think We Are? Imagining the New Britain*. London, United Kingdom: Allen Lane, 2000.

Bragg, Melvin. *The Adventure of English*. London, United Kingdom: Hodder & Stoughton, 2003.

Dorling Kindersley Children's Atlas. New York: DK Publishing, 2000.

Gunn, Simon and Rachel Bell. *The Middle Classes: Their Rise and Sprawl*. London, United Kingdom: Orion, 2002.

FILM

Elizabeth. Channel Four Films, 1998.

Four Weddings and a Funeral. Working Title Films, 1994.

A History of Britain—The Complete Collection. BBC/History Channel, 2000.

Monty Python's Flying Circus. BBC, 1969.

WEBSITES

10 Downing Street. www.number-10.gov.uk

Britannia: British History, Life, and Travel. www.britannia.com

British Broadcasting Corporation. www.bbc.co.uk

British Council. www.britishcouncil.org

British Monarchy. www.royal.gov.uk/output/page1.asp

BWEA—The British Wind Energy Association. www.bwea.com

Department for Environment, Food, and Rural Affairs. www.defra.gov.uk

Department of Trade and Industry. www.dti.gov.uk

Environment Agency. www.environment-agency.gov.uk

London. www.london.gov.uk

Manchester and the Northwest Region of England. www.manchester2002-UK.com

Manchester City Council. www.manchester.gov.uk

National Statistics Online. www.statistics.gov.uk

Spartacus Educational. www.spartacus.schoolnet.co.uk

Scottish Executive. www.scotland.gov.uk

Scottish Tourist Board. www.visitscotland.com

United Kingdom Parliament. www.parliament.uk

Tourist Information U.K. www.tourist-information-uk.com

Visit Britain. www.visitbritain.com

Wales Office. www.walesoffice.gov.uk

BIBLIOGRAPHY

Bryson, Bill. *Notes from a Small Island*. London, United Kingdom: Black Swan, 1996.

Hiro, Dilip. *Black British, White British: A History of Race Relations in Britain*. London, United Kingdom: Grafton, 1991.

Isaacs, Alan and Jennifer Monk (editors). *The Cambridge Illustrated Dictionary of British Heritage*. Cambridge, United Kingdom: Cambridge University Press, 1986.

James, Bill and Dennis Kavanagh. *British Politics Today*. Manchester, United Kingdom: Manchester University Press, 2003.

Kearney, Hugh. *The British Isles: A History of Four Nations*. Cambridge, United Kingdom: Cambridge University Press, 1989.

Mandelson, Peter and Roger Liddle. *The Blair Revolution Revisited*. London, United Kingdom: Politico's Publishing, 2002.

McDowell, David. *An Illustrated History of Britain*. London, United Kingdom: Longman, 1989.

Paxman, Jeremy. *Friends in High Places: Who Runs Britain?* London, United Kingdom: Penguin, 1991.

Williams, Roger (editor). *Great Britain*. Hong Kong: Insight Guides, APA Publications Ltd, 1992.

INDEX